ONCE A MARINE—
ALWAYS A MARINE

ONCE A MARINE—
ALWAYS A MARINE

BEN FINNEY

Foreword by
LEM SHEPHERD
GENERAL, UNITED STATES MARINE CORPS, (RET.)

CROWN PUBLISHERS, INC.
NEW YORK

Printed in the United States of America
Published simultaneously in Canada by General Publishing Company Ltd.

Library of Congress Cataloging in Publication Data

Finney, Ben, 1900–
  Once a marine—always a marine.

  1. Finney, Ben, 1900–   2. Soldiers—United States—Biography.   3.   United States. Marine Corps Reserve—Biography.   4.   United States. Marine Corps— History.   I. Title.
VE25.F56A34 1978   359.9'6'0924 [B] 77-15629
ISBN 0-517-53275-1

Second Printing, November 1978

DEDICATED TO

American men and women everywhere
who have served their country

CONTENTS

FOREWORD

Ben Finney's reminiscence, *Once a Marine–Always a Marine*, is a fascinating saga told by a raconteur who has few equals.

Descended from Virginia forebears who fought in America's War for Independence, Ben enlisted in the Marine Corps in 1917, while a student at Woodberry Forest School. Ordered to France, he joined the Fourth Marine Brigade, where he participated in combat as a member of my company.

Following the war, Ben maintained his interest in the Corps and was subsequently commissioned a reserve officer. In World War II, he served with Marine aviation in the Western Pacific and rose to the rank of lieutenant colonel. During the Korean conflict, he returned to active duty in the Far Eastern theater.

Between wars Ben, always an adventurous spirit, many times shot big game in Africa and India, and has known the great and near great from the four corners of the world.

In *Once a Marine–Always a Marine*, Ben tells with gung-ho enthusiasm and humor his experiences in three wars in his country's Corps of Soldiers of the Sea.

LEM SHEPHERD
General, United States Marine Corps (Ret.)

PREFACE

This is the story of a Marine reservist covering a period of forty-three years, from my Old Corps days on Parris Island to combat duty in three wars and up to my retirement in 1960. I fought my way through World War I, eased my way through World War II, and hated the Korean fiasco, a so-called war we should never have gotten into. We didn't lose—but we didn't win. I was able to ease my way through World War II mainly because I hadn't forgotten what I'd learned in the first "war to end all wars" and because many senior officers were in my age bracket.

From the periods between the wars, I have related some of my worldwide adventures.

I have tried not to play down America's other fighting forces—and I hope I haven't—because they deserve the highest praise. What th' hell. Together we won the war, didn't we?

1 | Once a Marine—
Always a Marine

IT WAS THE FALL OF 1917 AND THE UNITED STATES HAD become embroiled in the Great War that had been going on in Europe since July 1914.

I was a student at Woodberry Forest, a prep school near Orange, Virginia. During the Thanksgiving holidays, I dropped by the Marine recruiting office in Richmond to see what they had to offer a guy who had been on summer maneuvers with the Virginia National Guard.

The Marine Corps had recently acquired an island off the South Carolina coast to be used as an East Coast training base for enlistees, and the recruiting sergeant painted such a fabulous picture of Parris Island—beautiful beaches, swaying palm trees, and movies every night—that I could hardly wait to sign up. I was so sold that, when the sergeant said, "If you really want to enlist, and are not yet eighteen years of age, you must get a letter of permission from your parents," it posed no problem at all. I merely added a year to my actual age when I signed the enlistment papers. I saw no need to bother my father; all I wanted to do was help my country, if I could.

Two cousins of mine, who had just finished boot training at Parris Island and were then at Quantico, upon hearing that I was about to become a boot, came down from Quantico on the weekend before I was due to leave for Parris Island to offer some advice. They didn't actually say that the recruiting sergeant had been lying in his portrayal of Parris Island, but they most certainly intimated as much. What they did impress on me was how to be a good Marine: "Keep your hand down, your mouth shut, and be ready for anything."

Through the years, I found their advice to be all too true.

The recruiting office had supplied me with a railway ticket, which called for an early evening departure from Richmond and a predawn arrival at Yemassee, South Carolina, en route to Parris Island. When I detrained at Yemassee, a Marine came along with a flashlight and asked if I was headed for Parris Island. I told him I was, and he said, "Follow me."

We ended up in a ramshackle, canvas-covered affair where I was handed a towel and told to dry dishes. I was still drying dishes when someone announced that the train for Parris Island was being loaded. Along with five other soon-to-be-boots, I climbed aboard the passenger car of the two-car, narrow gauge train and was soon bumping along toward Port Royal. As we left the train, one of the chaps allowed as how it couldn't be our final destination, since it wasn't an island. And he was correct; a Marine corporal took us in tow and led us onto a pier and into a longboat. As the boat chugged its way toward Parris Island, I tried my best to spot at least one "beautiful beach," but all I could see was a line of bulrushes down to the water's edge. The longboat tied up to a wharf rigged in an old confederate dry dock, and we climbed ashore on Parris Island.

Virginia National Guard, Virginia Beach, summer 1915

2 | "Fabulous" Parris Island— and a Pig's Ankle

IT WAS APPARENT FROM SCRATCH THAT PARRIS ISLAND WAS a far cry from even a road-company Bermuda.

Lugging our suitcases through ankle-deep sand, under a scorching hot sun, we were led by a corporal to what was known then as "receiving camp," a barbed wire enclosure some two miles from our landing point. En route, I kept looking for swaying palm trees, but spotted only one or two. I learned later that most of them were clustered around officers' quarters. It became increasingly obvious that the sergeant in Richmond had sold me a bill of goods about "fabulous" Parris Island.

After a half-hour trek through the sand, wringing wet with perspiration, we approached receiving camp. On either side of the inner entrance, dozens of pajama-clad enlistees were lined up awaiting our arrival. One of them hollered, "Any of you guys from New York?" No answer. Another hollered, "Any of you guys from Connecticut?" Still no answer. Finally someone hollered, "Any of you from Virginia?" "Yeah," I answered. Whereupon all of the inmates yelled in accord, "You're sure out of luck!" An inspiring greeting!

New arrivals were led directly to the quartermaster's setup, where all civilian clothes were turned in and replaced with two suits of pajamas, both the same size. If you were big, they were tight; if you were small, they were loose—and that was that! No hat, no shoes. We were then taken to a barracks containing sixty-four cots and two small rooms, one for the drill instructor, the other for two corporals. Boot companies were made up of two platoons of four squads each—sixty-four men.

Every day started with a 4:30 reveille accompanied by a loud-mouthed corporal kicking cots and shouting, "Hit the deck, you bums." On the third day of barefoot torture, I had already started figuring how I could get out of the enclosure when I found myself lined up with a dozen or so fellow sufferers. A tough corporal barked at us, "Any of you bums ride a horse?" Horse, horse, I thought to myself, must mean a general's orderly. Completely forgetting my cousins' first bit of advice, I was carried away with the possibility of no longer having to trudge through loose sand. Up went my hand, along with three others.

"You four, two paces forward," barked the corporal. "Right face! Forward ho!" We were headed straight for the entrance gate, and I tripped along dreaming happily of the equestrian duties awaiting me when, just short of the gate, "Column, left!" redirected us to the rear of the camp galley.

"Detail, halt! Right face!" found us confronting a colossal pile of potatoes. "You see them spuds?" rasped the corporal. "Them's horses. Ride 'em!"

Hours later, the brown mountain had been reduced to several huge pails of blond potatoes. I turned to a fellow volunteer and remarked, "That's the last time I'll stick up my hand." He didn't even look up, but finally came back in a deep southern drawl, "You don't stick up your hand, you don't go no place. This time it led to 'taters, maybe next time to honey." His homespun philosophy might have been right, but I'll never know, because never again did I stick up my hand in the Marine Corps—unless I knew damned well what it was for.

Having signed enlistment papers in Richmond, I thought of myself as a full-fledged Marine, but that wasn't the way it worked. I found out that until an enlistee had passed a truly thorough physical examination at Parris Island, he wasn't considered a member of the Corps. And pajamas were the uniform of the day until the physical was passed. Those barefoot, sunburned, pajama-clad enlistees milling around waiting for their physicals were the most motley-looking group of patriotic Americans ever assembled.

One of the beautiful beaches I'd been told about was on the water side of receiving camp. It was far from beautiful and used only, as I found out, for testing the feet of prospective boots. I have high arches, but an overzealous corpsman figured I didn't, so for three hours I was made to walk up and down that damned beach, barefoot, with a sixty-pound pack on my back and a rifle on my shoulder. I passed the test, but could have killed that corpsman.

An eye-test gimmick of the physical exam was a large box containing literally hundreds of skeins of wool, all varying in color. Above the box hung three skeins of solid colors: red, green, and yellow. Every enlistee had to pick from the box three skeins that matched as nearly as possible each of the solid colors. As I neared this test, just ahead of me was a chap named Bennett, a trainmate from Yemassee. When he realized what was coming next, he turned and whispered, "Jesus! I'm color blind. Help me, will you?" "All right," I whispered back, "match the three colors in sequence, starting with the red. Every time you reach for a wrong shade, I'll nudge you." With my help, Bennett passed the test, and was as happy as a bird dog.

If he passed the physical, each boot was issued a campaign hat, two suits of fatigues, underwear, socks, and two pair of shoes. Later, I figured that the two pair of shoes had been issued in the very likely event that one pair would be worn out carrying buckets of oyster shells to build roads. We were also issued a blanket and a poncho. With the campaign hat adorned with the Marine emblem, the boots were at least beginning to look a bit more like Marines.

While the training company was being filled to its full complement, permanent squads of eight men each were being formed. When our drill instructor learned that I had attended Porter Military Academy and had been in the Virginia National Guard, he made me the "ackin-jack" of my squad. An ackin-jack was somewhere between a private and a corporal and is now known as a private first class or lance corporal. Having been made an ackin-jack turned out to be my first good break in the Corps because, when the full company was readying to shove off for its first go at actual training in an area then known as maneuver grounds, the drill instructor assigned me to see that the company's seabags were loaded in a truck and to ride herd on them. The company took off on its three-mile trek through the sand about half an hour before the truck was loaded. As the truck caught up and passed the perspiring group, Bennett spied me atop the seabags and, pointing his finger at me, shouted, "You son-of-a-bitch, you got me into this." Unappreciative, I call it.

On the flat sands of the maneuver grounds, we pitched pup tents and an attempt was started to turn us into Leathernecks. (The term *Leatherneck* was tagged on Marines by sailors in the early nineteenth century, when Marine blouses had leather collars. No one seems to remember just why, but the most accepted theory is that the collars forced their wearers to hold their heads erect. Another theory is that the collars afforded a certain protection in sword encounters.) Half of our daylight hours were spent on weapons training and endless marching. The other half was spent in building oyster shell roads. Nights were spent battling sand fleas. It was really rugged! My fellow scratcher in a pup tent was a chap named Jeff Downey. We were in the same squad until Saint-Mihiel.

A creek now called Ribbon Creek ran past the maneuver grounds. It is the creek that became notorious many years later, when Sergeant McKeon was accused of causing the death of several boots there. In the Old Corps days, the heads were built out over this creek, and we had another name for it.

Three weeks of maneuver grounds behind us, we trudged through the sand to the training camp, which was located more or less across the parade ground from the main barracks. Our company moved into one of a series of bunkhouses. That lying sergeant in Richmond had said there were nightly movies at training camp. There were nightly movies all right, but only for noncoms. Mere boots simply climbed into their cots and wished they were somewhere else.

Mentioning climbing onto cots reminds me of something that happened during our first few nights in the training-camp bunkhouse. I pass it along as fairly conclusive proof that when men are headed for battle they are very apt to pray a little harder.

For as long as I can remember, I have always gotten on my knees to say my prayers. The first night in the bunkhouse, I was all pooped out and readied myself to climb onto my cot before taps and lights out. As I got on my knees to say my prayers, conversation around me eased a bit, but I could plainly hear titters. The next night, I noticed several other men on their knees. Conversation practically stopped, and only a few titters were heard here and there. On the third night, the majority of the men in the bunkhouse were on their knees, and hardly a sound of any kind could be heard. War changes a lot of things.

Intensive drilling was the order of the day—that is, unless we were ordered to unload lumber from barges tied up to docks in a creek near our bunkhouse. And then came the rifle range, which was just across a creek from the receiving camp. Every morning for three weeks, we would hike to the range shortly after daylight and spend the day pulling targets up and down in the butts, sighting-in, shooting, or just sitting in the sun waiting for the day we would shoot for record. By now, our fatigues were distinctly showing wear and tear. The drill instructor told us to pick our worst-looking coat, cut off the sleeves at the elbows, and cut slits down both sides under the armholes. This, he told us, would make us more comfortable when shooting. Now we really looked like a bunch of bums. People used to seeing Marines in dress blues would have found it hard to believe that they ever looked like we did.

Sometimes we were allowed to cross a foot bridge to the receiving camp for a cold Coke at the PX. One day, while having a Coke, I ran into a newly arrived, pajama-clad friend of mine from Richmond. When he saw the cut-up, anything-but-Marine-looking outfit I had on, he bleated, "Good God! Do they do that to you? I'm getting the hell out of here." I started to tell him that he had about as much chance as a bastard at a family reunion, but I didn't.

After about a week on the range, a group of us were sitting around awaiting our turn in the butts when one of the group said, "You know something? Qualifying here on the range could be extremely important." "What do you mean?" he was asked. "Well, you know what I heard? I heard it rumored that if a boot doesn't qualify, he is kept on Parris Island as a cook." "What did you say?" I quickly asked. When he repeated what he had heard, I picked up my rifle and began sighting-in on my own. I had taken rifle-shooting

Quantico, 1918

in a lackadaisical sort of way, but I quickly changed. I didn't know if the rumor was right or wrong, but I wasn't a cook and didn't want to be, so I was taking no chances. I ended up second high gun in the company!

Three months to the day after I'd landed on Parris Island, I was shipped to Quantico. I must admit that I had tears in my eyes as my train passed through the center of Richmond, within blocks of a home that had never left my thoughts.

Our intensive training continued at Quantico and included our being taught how to string barbed wire and dig trenches in a burned-over area some three miles west of the base. It was at Quantico that I first heard the term *lace-pants Marine*. It was tagged on Marines who had booted at Mare Island, the West Coast training base near San Francisco, by Parris Island graduates.

3 | The Hard Way

AFTER A MONTH OF TOUGH MARINE TRAINING AT QUAN-tico, as I stood on a dock at League Island, Philadelphia, waiting to be herded aboard the Marine transport *Henderson,* I saw a familiar figure threading his way toward me through the restricted area. It was my father! He gave me a small bear hug and pressed a package in my hand. "This might come in handy, kid," was all he said. A few minutes later we mounted the gangway. It was not until I had found a

Jeff Downey and the author, France, 1918

bunk in the bowels of the ship and stowed my gear that I had a chance to open the package. It was a money belt containing $500, more cash than I'd ever seen at one time in my life.

This windfall had been observed by a character who lay stretched out on a bunk near mine. He hoisted himself on one elbow and casually suggested, "Let's you and me have a little action. How about some blackjack?"

I hadn't played too much blackjack, I was a crap-shooter, but how could a guy with 500 bucks lose? So I answered, "Why not?" We found a secluded section of the hold and started playing. There were some kibitzers watching, among them Shorty Long, an old man of about thirty and senior member of the platoon. The game was short—and disastrous. The *Henderson* hadn't cleared the mouth of the Delaware River before I was flat broke!

Later, I was standing at a deck rail in a numbed condition when Shorty Long ranged alongside. "How long you been playing blackjack, boy?" he asked. "Not long enough, I guess," I replied. "That figures," he said. "Come below and I'll show you how that guy took you." Back in the hold, Shorty demonstrated how he could bank dice against the bulkhead and call the turn five out of six times. He then borrowed a deck of cards and proceeded to show me how he could shuffle it, cut it, and deal any card he wished. "That's how it happened," explained Shorty who, it turned out, had operated a gambling joint in East St. Louis and had good reason to know all the angles, legitimate or otherwise.

The more I thought of how I'd been taken, the madder I got. "I think I'll kill that son-of-a-bitch," I said. Putting a friendly hand on my shoulder, Shorty said, "Take it easy, boy. I'll try and get your dough back for you. Take this twenty bucks and bet with me in any game I'm in." I did, and not only got my five hundred back—I got more. And don't think it didn't come in handy. During my entire sojourn in France, I received not one paycheck from Washington, or anywhere. I guess the postmen didn't like to be shot at.

In one crap game aboard the *Henderson,* a guy ran out of real money and offered to shoot twenty ten-dollar bills of the confederate variety against ten Yankee dollars. Although it struck me as an insult to the South, I faded him and won. I tucked the twenty tens into my pack, never dreaming how handy the devalued money would be one day soon.

By the time our platoon got to Europe, the war had really revved into high gear. The French had even commandeered Paris taxicabs to hasten troops to the front, in an effort to try and stop the German invasion.

After landing on the outskirts of Saint-Nazaire, our outfit pitched camp in a field surrounded by a thick hedge, and we were allowed no liberty. After dark, a French face would appear in a break in the hedge, a bottle would be offered and, after some haggling, exchanged for American money.

The going prices were ridiculously high. Sometimes, the asking price was eight or ten times more than the same bottle would have cost in a liquor store. Finally, I took charge of one of the exchange posts and bought enough brandy with my confederate money to keep the entire company plastered for days. I have often wondered what happened when those dollar-grabbing Frenchmen tried to change that southern money into francs.

We did get into the city of Saint-Nazaire once, to help unload ships tied up to its docks. So many chock-full packs were brought back from the ships, the powers-that-be decided they wouldn't need us again. They probably figured we might steal the docks. But the stuff brought back to camp in the packs made for excellent bargaining with the faces in the hedges.

Then, all of a sudden, sixty-odd Marines were crammed in an antiquated boxcar designed to hold forty men or eight horses, and off we rattled to join the Fifth Marine Regiment, Second Division, Allied Expeditionary Force.

It didn't take long to find out that American cigarettes in the Fifth Regiment were hard to come by, and the English cigarettes sometimes available were hardly worth coming by. So, when the Salvation Army came up with Bull Durham, I decided to become a "roll-your-owner." Anyone who wants to smoke badly enough can learn to roll a cigarette. Admittedly, I wasted most of my first sack of tobacco learning, but by the end of the war I could roll a cigarette blindfolded.

Mentioning a hand-rolled cigarette reminds me of something that happened recently. After lunch one day, I started "rolling one," and my luncheon companion asked me how much money I had saved smoking Bull Durham. I told him I didn't know, but his question intrigued me so much that I figured it out as well as I could.

During the nearly sixty years since World War I, I have smoked an average of one sack of Bull Durham per day, from which I get about forty cigarettes, the equivalent of two packs of manufactured cigarettes. Through the years, my Bull Durham has cost me six cents a sack, more or less, a total of $21.60 per year. For the same length of time, two packs of manufactured cigarettes, including those bought from pretty cigarette girls, would have averaged around thirty cents per pack, or $216 per year. Over the period, the cost of packaged cigarettes would add up to $12,528, whereas my Bull Durham has cost but $1,253! I was astounded when I realized that I must have saved over $11,000 by smoking Bull Durham. I am now trying my damndest to figure out where in hell my saving went and, I might add, getting exactly nowhere. I can only conjecture that it went up in smoke.

While on the subject of tobacco, it behooves me to pass along the findings of a doctor friend of mine who is a fanatic on the so-called ills caused by smoking ready-made cigarettes. Right or wrong, he contends that the average manufactured cigarette contains 3.2 or 3.3 percent nicotine tar, while a cigarette rolled with pure tobacco, in a rice-straw paper with no glue thereon, contains only .03 percent nicotine tar. He goes on to point out that a manufactured cigarette contains glycerine to keep the tobacco moist, saltpeter to keep it burning, and is rolled with inferior paper. I have no idea if my friend is correct or not, but even if he is only half correct, I intend to keep on smoking Bull Durham and Riz La Croix papers.

I had been smoking "makins" for a week or so when the battle of Soissons reared its ugly head. In the Great War, along with Chateau-Thierry and Belleau Wood, Soissons can be considered a turning point for the Allies from defensive to offensive warfare.

With Heinie shells bursting like crazy all around us, I was cuddled up in a shellhole with three other gyrenes. With nothing else to do, I decided to show off the deftness of my fingers and had about finished "rolling one" when a near-miss burst close to our hole. A chap facing me asked, "You aren't nervous, are you?" "Not me," I replied. "Why'd you ask?" "Look at your cigarette," he suggested. I looked down at my effort to find that I was rolling not a bloody thing but paper!

Between Soissons and the Saint-Mihiel show, things were fairly dull. When I noticed a couple of soldiers unloading a truck, I asked them where they were headed. "Back to Paris," they answered. I talked real fast and persuaded them to let me hide in the truck and hitch a ride to Paris.

On my second day in Paris, I ran into Sergeant Henry Topping, the father of Dan Topping, who later owned the New York Yankees. Henry was a chauffeur for some Army general stationed in Paris. At the moment, Henry's general was out of town, and Henry was celebrating his absence with a few drinks. The least I could do was to help him, with the result that, come midnight, we were both pretty wobbly. As we reeled down the Champs Elysées, we passed a large, unprotected plate-glass store window. Looking at the window, Henry said, "I wonder how much noise it would make if we kicked in that window." "Why don't we find out?" I came back, and WHAM! We kicked at the same time. The answer to Henry's implied question was—a hell of a lot. Pieces of glass shattered down, some on the sidewalk. That accomplished, we staggered on as far as the corner, where two MPs grabbed us. We were taken to Sainte-Anne prison, located in the Military Police headquarters on Rue Sainte-Anne, where they wanted to see our dog tags. My AWOL status had caused me to carefully hide mine in a sock. Henry mentioned the name of his general and talked them into letting him call one of the general's aides. Henry and I then went to sleep. The aide contacted must have been beholden to Henry, for by early dawn he had effected our release, after guaranteeing that we would pay for replacing the window. By train and truck I wangled my way back to my outfit and was glad to find that, in the topsy-turvy condition between fronts, I'd hardly been missed.

By no means do I intend to imply that my behavior in the foregoing story was typical of a career Marine. Things like that happened in all branches of the military, if a guy thought he could get away with it. Don't forget, I was young, a reservist, and wanted to see Paris.

About six weeks after Soissons came Saint-Mihiel, the first completely American operation of the war, where American troops more than proved their worth as combatants. In pitch darkness on the night of September 11, 1918, my company was deployed in front of the enemy lines preparatory to "going over" at daylight. Not being able to locate what I considered a deep enough shellhole, I sauntered off some forty or fifty yards to the side, trying to find one. All of a sudden, BOOM!—an American artillery unit I hadn't known was there let go a salvo right over my head! Within seconds I had rejoined my company, broken out my shovel, and was off for China.

Compared to other battles, Saint-Mihiel wasn't too rugged, but it was tough on Jeff Downey, who caught a piece of high explosive in his shoulder and had to be evacuated. Maybe he was lucky because, following Saint-Mihiel, we ran into a real rough show, Mont Blanc Ridge, in the Champagne sector. The Fifth and Sixth Marine Regiments were assigned to do something—and did—that the Allies hadn't been able to do in four years: capture Mont Blanc Ridge and the cathedral thereon.

When the ridge was secured, I was one of a detail sent out to rig barbed wire on the German side of the trenches. The detail must have been spotted by the Heinies because suddenly shells started bursting right on us. A small piece of shrapnel pierced the front of my tin hat, and blood started oozing from my forehead. Barrage or no barrage, I crawled back to the trench, dove in, and looked for a first aid station. Finding one, I pushed my way through really badly wounded men in an effort to locate a corpsman. I found one all right, the same son-of-a-bitch that had thought I had flat feet on Parris Island. Figuring that I'd rather bleed to death than have that bastard touch me, I found a piece of gauze, mopped my forehead, and looked in a broken mirror. What I saw was an inconsequential gash down my forehead. Obviously, all that happened was a sharp point of my punctured tin hat had cut my forehead.

Feeling like a cowardly jerk, I climbed out of the trench and crawled my way back to the detail. About ten minutes later, I wished to hell I hadn't when fragments of high explosive embedded themselves in both knees, completely immobilizing me. When artillery fire let up, stretcher bearers carried me back to a first aid station, where two small pieces of metal were removed and my knees bandaged. Later, an ambulance took me to an evacuation tent-hospital in the village of Sompey.

Within two weeks, the bandage was off my left knee, and my right knee, although still bandaged, was so much better I was beginning to wonder what I could do about finding my outfit. While I was sitting in front of my tent one day, a Marine driving a small truck stopped and asked me where he could find the Fifth Regiment. "I wish to God I knew," I told him, and then said, "If you'll wait 'til I fetch my gear, I'll help you find it." On October 30, we ran down the Fifth Regiment, dug in on the western edge of the Argonne Forest and ready to get under way for the climactic last offensive of the war.

Starting in the early morning of October 31 and for twenty-four hours thereafter, the Allies laid down the heaviest artillery barrage of the war. After dark, even French 75s were wheeled into position between our deployed troops and the German line. It was the Sixth Regiment's turn to "go over" first, so by the time the Fifth reached the top of the hill where the Germans had been entrenched, there weren't many prisoners left to be taken. The Fourth Marine Brigade's sector was roughly between the two small towns of Saint-Georges and Landes-Saint-Georges, both some two miles farther toward Germany from the top of the hill. We watched as our artillery turned the towns into rubble.

Just before we were about to take off after the Germans, I

could tell that my bandage had loosened and, unable to raise my pants leg because of wrap puttees, I let down my pants and was starting to tighten the bandage. Just then, my sergeant walked by and said, "I didn't know you had anything wrong with your ass, Finney. I thought it was your knee. You'd better take it easy. Catch up with us when you can." I never argued with sergeants, so I did exactly what he had told me to do. I curled up in what was left of a German dugout and went to sleep. And going to sleep was no problem after having heard continuous cannon fire for twenty-four hours.

In the early afternoon, I was awakened by some bum who fell in the dugout on top of me. I took off after my company. I can't say I was exactly running, as my handicapped knee wouldn't let me. Otherwise I might have been. Darkness fell, and I still hadn't caught up with my outfit. After dining on half a tin of corned beef, nicknamed "tinned willie," and crackers, I wrapped my poncho around me and bedded down for the night among the limbs of a fallen tree.

Following a breakfast of "tinned willie" and crackers, I continued my chase. Around noon, I ran into a French light artillery outfit that was having chow. I dug out my mess kit and joined them. After I'd rolled a "makins" for the chef, he dished me up a second helping of a kind of stew. It was more filling than tasty, but anything would have tasted better than that damned "tinned willie." I might add that since World War I, never have I endeavored to find tinned corned beef on grocer's shelves.

Leaving the Frenchmen, I crossed a small, open area in the middle of which was a young German officer with a badly shattered leg. He couldn't even get up, let alone walk. He spoke no English, which matched my ability to speak German, so conversation was automatically eliminated. But feeling sorry for the guy, I broke out my first aid kit, poured a small bottle of Dakin's solution on his leg, and bandaged it. He must have appreciated my effort, because when I was ready to carry on, he reached in his blouse, pulled out a

Luger, and handed it to me by the barrel. I took it, and when I found out that it was fully loaded, I wondered what might have happened if I'd known that he had it. It could have been that the following story would have died a-bornin'.

4 | An Incredible
Coincidence

I DIGRESS HERE TO PUSH TIME FORWARD FROM NOVEMBER 1918 to August 1922 when, after a trip up the Rhine from Cologne to Coblenz, I decided that instead of returning to Paris I'd have a look at Berlin. The value of the German mark had so drastically weakened, it seemed as though American pennies had turned into pure gold, and that was certainly a propitious moment for an American to visit Germany. As an example: most drinks at the Adlon Bar, probably the most expensive bar in Berlin, cost the equivalent of less than one half a cent, and my suite at the Adlon cost less than a dollar a day. It was impossible for stores to mark up their prices to keep pace with the falling mark, making shopping a distinct pleasure.

On my second day in Berlin, I visited the Berlin Police Kennel, where I saw the most beautiful dog I'd ever seen. He was a German shepherd named Egon von Grimnitz and the show dog of the kennel. That figured, as he had won best in show at the first dog show in Berlin after World War I. The following day, and the next, and the next, for three weeks, I visited the kennel and tried to purchase Egon. No soap. However, as the mark continued to look weaker and weaker and my dollars stronger and stronger, the police finally accepted my offer, and Egon was mine. I can't ever remember being happier. Through the following years, Egon was my good friend and constant companion.

Apparently, the sale of Egon was of enough importance to be carried in the Berlin papers the next day. My floor captain, who could speak English, brought the morning paper with my breakfast and read me the story therein. It contained the fact that the champion, Egon von Grimnitz, had been sold to an American named Finney, who was presently a guest at the Adlon Hotel.

Shortly before noon, a call from the front desk informed me that Herr Berghoff would like to see me. I didn't know anyone named Berghoff, but thinking it might have something to do with Egon, I told the desk to send him up, and then locked Egon in the bedroom. Within a couple of minutes, there was a knock on the door and in walked—believe it or not—the wounded German officer I had helped in the Argonne nearly four years before! I was so dumbfounded all I could say was, "How in the world did you find me?" "I saw your name in the morning paper," he answered. "I know, so did I," I said, "but how did you know my name?" "I saw the name *Finney* on your first aid kit the day you saved my life and wanted to thank you again." When I asked him how he had acquired his command of

Egon von Grimnitz

English, he told me that he had married an English-speaking Dutch gal who liked to show off her mastery of the English language at the slightest provocation. He went on to say that she had practically forced him to learn how to speak English. Over a bottle of schnapps, we agreed how nice it was to be out of uniforms and how sincerely much we hoped that we would never have to don them again.

By now, it was Hans and Ben. When I told Hans that Egon and I were leaving for Vienna the next day, he insisted that I have dinner at his home that evening. His wife, Helga, turned out to be a very charming gal, and his mother, very nice. And that ended a million to one coincidence. Not exactly "ended," because on subsequent visits to Berlin in 1928 and 1932 I saw a lot of the Berghoffs. In 1932 I spent two weekends with them at their cottage on the shore of a lake near Berlin. In 1935, the coincidence really ended when I received a letter from Helga, postmarked Amsterdam, telling me that Hans had been killed in a motor accident.

Egon advertising his adopted homeland, 1924

5 | Three Days before the Armistice

GETTING BACK TO THE LAST DAYS OF THE GREAT WAR—I caught up with my battalion on the west bank of the Meuse River, where they were waiting to see what was going to happen. Shooting was sparse, as nobody seemed to be certain just who was where. En route to the Meuse, the Fourth Brigade had surprised a German artillery battery still shooting away, not knowing that their foot-soldiers were behind them, on their way to Berlin.

In the early morning hours of November 8, a boatload of Marines was sent across the Meuse to pick out the most likely spot for the eastern end of a pontoon bridge. I was one of the boatload. Having found the best spot to anchor a bridgehead, we were preparing to recross the river when all hell broke loose. The Heinies must have thought a whole division was on their side of the Meuse, because they laid down on us what could have been the last barrage of the war. I dove into a brand-new shell hole, broke out my pack shovel, and again was on my way to China. I might point out here that, under shellfire, I was probably the fastest and deepest digger in the Marine Corps. If Heinie shells were landing close, I could dig faster with a spoon than the average Marine could with a shovel. Sometimes I dug so deep, a rope would have to be lowered to help me get out. And once, I dug so deep I thought I could hear Chinese being spoken below me. I hadn't gotten far below the surface when I detected the distinct sound of a gas shell. Forgetting China, and with the speed of sound, I dug out my gas mask and had it halfway on when a mustard gas shell burst, practically in the shell hole with me. I passed out.

The next thing I remembered with any clarity was coming to on a bunk in a hospital car. The train had stopped, and outside I could hear bells ringing, horns blowing, and people hysterically screaming what sounded like: "Finney! Finney!" Figuring that I had done something I didn't know about and was being acknowledged as some kind of hero, I crawled painfully out of my bunk. Although I was a walking basket case, my tongue as big as a small orange and badly burned between my legs and under my arms by the gas, I staggered to the half-open Dutch door in the middle of the car, and stood there awaiting the plaudits of my public. It was then that I clearly heard what they were actually yelling: *"Finie! Finie! La guerre est finie."*

It was Armistice Day!

Wondering where I was going, I asked one of the car's attendants who told me that the occupants of my particular car were headed for Base Hospital 6 in Limoges. Upon our arrival at Limoges, ambulances took us to the DeHaviland china factory, in which Base 6 was located. I ended up in a large ward containing forty or more beds, where I was kept for two months.

Sometime around Christmas, a distant relative of mine, Dr. J.M.T. Finney who was commanding general of Base Hospital 1 in Paris, arrived at Base 6 on an inspection trip. While there, he dropped by my ward to say hello. A general in a ward caused quite a furor. (I relate the foregoing incident because of something that happened two wars later, in Korea.)

In mid-January, I was shipped to an evacuation hospital in Bassens, the port of Bordeaux near the mouth of the Gironde River. Four or five days later, I was loaded aboard the U.S.S. *Siboney,* an ocean liner of sorts converted into a hospital ship. The trip across the Atlantic was wonderful, mainly because we were headed in a westerly direction. When we docked at Hoboken, ambulances from Brooklyn Naval Hospital were waiting for us. For the next four months, doctors at the hospital tried to ascertain the seriousness of the apices on my lungs (whatever they were) caused by the mustard gas.

For the last half of the four months, I was transferred to an old Hudson River Line boat that had been converted into a hospital ship and tied up to a dock at the East River end of Fourteenth Street. I can't remember more than six or seven patients ever having been in the "hospital" at any one time, and, unless we had to report to Brooklyn, we could come and go as we pleased. After the baseball season opened, most of my afternoons were spent at the Polo Grounds or Ebbetts Field and many nights at either Rector's, Tony Pastor's, or maybe Webster Hall.

Finally, on May 31, 1919, I was given a disability discharge and high-tailed it for Virginia.

6 | In Between Wars

THE FOLLOWING SEPTEMBER, I ENROLLED IN THE UNIVERsity of Virginia. I lasted there as long as I did through the good graces of Dean Page, who was partial to veterans and a friend of my father, who was at the time president of the University of the South at Sewanee, Tennessee.

When I was a boy, my father had expressed his hopes more than once that I would grow up to be a Christian gentleman, to go to Sewanee, and to join the Alpha Tau

Omega fraternity, of which he was later the national president. I like to think I was still working on his first hope when I entered The University of Virginia. That knocked off his second hope, and his third was shot to hell when I pledged to join the Beta Theta Pi fraternity. Many of my Woodberry Forest chums were Betas.

As one of the Beta initiation gimmicks I was locked up from midnight to dawn in the West Range room Edgar Allan Poe had occupied while a student at the university. The story going the rounds was that Poe's ghost would show up in the room to dissuade intruders. All electricity had been disconnected, and, obviously rigged by my initiators, gadgets scraped on the door, rattled the shutters, and tapped on the walls. Imagine! Thinking such foolishness would frighten a guy who a year before had been up to his ass in hostile Germans. In any event, if Poe's ghost was around I didn't see it, because I slept like a baby.

However, they came up with another gimmick that would have humiliated anybody. For three hours, I had to sit on the front seat of a trolley car, keep my mouth shut, and whittle on a hard-boiled egg. What's more, I had to make the egg last for three hours. Please don't get the impression that I didn't love the university, because I did, but just before the Christmas holidays of 1922, I left and moved to North Carolina to live.

In January 1924, I rented a house in Miami Beach. During the day of the night I was having a housewarming party, I ran into Alan Crosland and asked him to attend. "I'd love to," he said. "Would you mind if I bring Betty Compson with me? She's the leading lady in a movie we're about to start shooting, called *Miami*." Late in the evening, when the party was pretty well wetted down, Betty Compson asked Alan, "Why do we have to get that leading man down from New York? What about Ben?" Turning to me, Alan asked, "Would you like to be in movies?" "Sure," I answered, not being at all sure of what he was talking about.

Two mornings later, at seven o'clock, someone mashed

Still shot with Betty Compson, Miami, *1924*

the front door bell. Poking my head out of an upstairs window, I asked, "What do you want?" "I came to pick you up," the man at the front door answered. "What th' hell for?" I hollered. "To take you to the Hialeah Studio," he came back. Then I remembered Alan's question. Within an hour after I arrived at the studio, I was made up and facing the first movie camera I had ever seen in my life. My German shepherd, Egon, was used early in the picture and gradually written more and more into the script. He turned out to be the best thing in the film!

I'll have you know that Regina Cannon, in her review of the film, had this to say, "Ben Finney has all the makings of a cinema success. He possesses the charm of Tommy

Meighan, the good fellowship of Richard Dix, and the sex appeal of Valentino. Quite a large order for one he-man, you say? Well, be that as it may, our hero fills it." Her review ended, and again I quote, "Success, Ben Finney, and when your name goes up in electrics, we'll be among the first to say: 'We told you so!'" Maybe I should have had a try at movies. But on the other hand, if I had, I would have missed some marvelous adventures, and even before *Miami* had finished being filmed, I had decided that movies were not for me. The day after a completion party at the studio, remembering April in Paris, Egon and I were off for France.

Most people arriving in Paris late at night go directly to a hotel and go to bed. I didn't. I went straight to Joe Zelli's, and, while Egon waited in the coatroom, I drank pop until well after daylight. And the same thing went on night after night.

Most of my daylight hours were spent in the Ritz Bar on the Rue Cambon practicing for my nighttime guzzling, but sometimes I would cross the Seine to visit the Rotonde bar and restaurant, a favorite Left Bank gathering place for

Scott Fitzgerald, Riviera, 1926

transplanted Americans like Scott Fitzgerald and Cole Porter. Scott was living alone in an apartment not far from the Rotonde, Cole and his bride in a home near the Invalides. Mentioning Scott reminds me of his "invention."

One day after Scott and I had lunched at the Rotonde, he suggested that I accompany him to his apartment as he had an invention he wanted me to see. At his apartment, I was looking through the window in his rather small living room at the bright sunshine outside when suddenly water started running down the windowpanes. Still wondering where the rain had come from, I asked, "What about your invention?" Scott replied, "You're looking at it. Watch." With that he reached under a corner of a couch, turned something, and the water stopped. "What th' hell kind of an invention is that?" I asked. His explanation: "You know how it is, Ole Boy, it's much easier to persuade a gal not to leave if it's raining."

At the end of a month or so I was becoming increasingly certain that I was overdoing it. So one evening, while dining with Cole Porter at his Left Bank home, I asked him if he happened to know of some spot I could get away from it all and rest up. He thought for a moment, and then asked me if I'd ever heard of Barbizon, a small town on the edge of the forest of Fontainebleau, some sixty kilometers south of Paris. He continued, "There's a small hostelry in the town called the Bas Breu that I think is exactly the sort of spot you are looking for. Practically no drinking. Nice and quiet."

Egon and I didn't arrive at the Bas Breu until the next afternoon. We were escorted through an open courtyard to our room. There was only one person in the courtyard, a fairly large, athletic-looking man sitting at one of the tables. After stowing my gear I returned to the courtyard. As I did, the man at the table asked me in a loud voice if I knew how to make a mint julep. "Certainly I do. I'm from Virginia!" I answered. "I don't give a damn if you're from the Ides of March," he came back, "if you know how to make a julep. There's a big bed of mint over there, and I've got a case of damned good bourbon [hard to get in France], but these Frog bastards don't know what a julep is, let alone how to concoct one." "Break out the bourbon while I cut some mint. Your problem is solved," I told him. I made so many juleps, the Frogs learned the knack, and from then on it was simply a case of Ernest Hemingway and I sitting still and sticking our noses in mint.

When Ernest told me he was living in the same room that Robert Louis Stevenson had occupied while writing *Treasure Island*, I accused him of having chosen that room in hopes that some of Stevenson's talent would rub off on him. His answer: "Could be!" Ernest's hope was certainly achieved—and then some.

At the end of four days, there was an elegant sufficiency of mint left, but a case of good bourbon lasts only so long. The fact that we were down to the last half a bottle didn't hasten my return to Paris as much as the look on Egon's face. It seemed to be asking, "Are you some kind of nut?" I realized that Egon missed Zelli's coatroom, so, naturally, we visited Joe Zelli on our first night back in Paris.

This is a propitious spot to pass along a real honest-to-God Virginia mint julep recipe that has been in my family for generations. If you follow it meticulously, you'll have the best mint julep you ever raised to your lips.

Practically everybody has heard of a mint julep, but very few mixologists know how to concoct one properly. Mint juleps originated in Williamsburg, Virginia, back in the seventeenth century, and the original recipe has never been bettered. Here 'tis.

Break, and drop into a dry, 10-ounce silver or pewter tankard, *with handle*, 15 or 20 (depending on the size of the leaves) *fresh*, I repeat, *fresh* mint leaves. Add a scant half teaspoon of granulated sugar and two tablespoons of water. Then muddle the leaves until they are well crushed and the sugar is dissolved. Pack the tankard with finely crushed ice. Pour (not measure) enough bourbon into the tankard to come to about an inch below the rim. After *thoroughly* stirring, add crushed ice up to the rim and float thereon a teaspoon of Barbados rum. Insert 2 large, or 3 small, sprigs of mint to the right of the handle, allowing the mint to protrude 2 inches above the rim. When imbibing, shove your nose into the protruding mint and sniff and quaff at the same time. Oh Boy! My mouth is watering. I've found that the ideal main ingredient in a julep is a 90-proof sour mash bourbon. I've also found that light Mount Gay rum makes an excellent float.

If you possess only an 8-ounce tankard, don't worry. The above recipe applies. If you are expecting visitors, whip up enough juleps and place them in the freezer for not more than half an hour before serving. Or, if you are expecting quite a few guests, I suggest that you prepare beforehand a mash of muddled mint leaves, sugar, and water, always adhering strictly to the proportions in the recipe. Also, it would save time if you readied the sprigs of mint in which your guests will stick their noses. If you insist on starting with a frosted tankard, all right. Personally, I find it difficult to wait for a tankard to frost, and it does anyway when you stir the ice and mint. Actually, a frosted tankard doesn't enhance the taste of the nectar one whit. It just makes it look better.

It is a known fact that the State of Kentucky prides itself on its bourbon, and it should, because Kentucky bourbon is a good whiskey. However, there is one thing for real sure: when Daniel Boone left Virginia and headed west across the Blue Ridge, he definitely did not take a Virginia mint julep recipe with him. And what's more, it is a crying shame that the "things" served at Churchill Downs on Derby Day are allowed to be called mint juleps. If they are the only "juleps" you have ever tasted, you still haven't ever tasted a mint julep.

Although my julep-guzzling at the Bas Breu contributed absolutely nothing to my well-being, it did establish a friendship between Ernest and me that lasted for many years—in Antibes, New York, Bimini, and Cuba. Once when I was visiting him at his home in San Francisco de

The author and Ernest Hemingway, Bimini, 1934

Paula, east of Havana, he was writing *For Whom the Bell Tolls*. He would arise about four o'clock in the morning and start writing, in order to have more daylight hours to spend fishing from his beloved boat, the *Pilar*. He wrote in long-hand, standing at an easel. I remember asking him, "Why?" His answer: "It helps keep me awake." I would come down for breakfast around seven and he would pass over to me his morning's output to read. One morning it was about Jordan and Maria's affair in a sleeping bag. It was so realistic that at one point I had reason, shall we say, to readjust myself. Ernest noticed my reaction and ejaculated, "It'll sell!" When Mary Welch changed her last name to Hemingway in 1946, I attended their wedding in Havana. Years later, in what turned out to be Ernest's last birthday spent aboard the *Pilar,* he and Mary asked me to join them. Ernest and I were trolling lines, both baited for white marlin. I got a strike and boated a marlin. After lunch ending with birthday cake and champagne, I had another strike on my line and boated a fish. (Ernest hadn't had even a nibble.) Whereupon, in a loud voice he asked, "Who th' hell's birthday is this?" I raised my glass to him. Wish I could do it again.

Ernest's son Bumby, Ernest, and myself, Bimini, 1937

Between 1925 and 1931, I traveled around the world six times, with two- to three-month stopovers in Shanghai on each trip, followed on four occasions with shikars or safaris in Indochina, India or Africa. One of our base camps in Indochina, just east of Bien Me Thot on the Laotian border, was later bisected by the Ho Chi Minh trail. On several trips, I made a point of visiting the fabulous ruins at Angkor which, to me, are truly the eighth wonder of the world.

I think I'd be amiss if I didn't mention that each summer was spent at the Hotel du Cap on Cap D'Antibes. It happened completely inadvertently. Returning from the Orient in 1926 for another April in Paris, I joined the round-the-world cruise ship *Belgenland* in Bombay and disembarked at Monte Carlo. As the Train Bleu didn't leave for Paris until the afternoon, I decided to motor over to the Hotel du Cap for lunch and pick it up in Cannes.

After I had had a delightful lunch on the terrace of the hotel, a young man approached my table and asked if I would like to look around the grounds. The young man was André Sella, son of the owner, and he had just taken over as head man. We started our tour by walking down a wide, gravelled roadway to what was known as the Top of the Rocks at Eden Roc, overlooking the bathing rocks and clear blue water below.

Soochow Creek, Shanghai, 1925

Thirteen Club, Shanghai, 1926

Duck shooting, Yangtze River, China, 1928

When I saw that water, our tour ended right there. "You wouldn't happen to know where I could find a pair of bathing trunks, would you?" Whereupon Sella disappeared into the basement of the pavilion and reappeared shortly, holding up a pair of trunks. "You can change in here," he said. I dived from the rocks and swam around for half an hour or more, and thoroughly enjoyed it. Returning to the Top of the Rocks, I sat at a table with Sella while I dried myself. In the distance, across Golfe-Juan, could be seen the still-snow-covered peaks of the Alpes Maritimes. It was a really beautiful sight. In our conversation, André asked me how long I had been coming to France. When I told him, "Ever since World War I, when I came with the Marines," I thought he looked a bit impressed, but I didn't know why. I said: "Those rocks must be covered with people in midsummer." "There's nobody on the rocks in midsummer," he replied.

Tea planter from Sarawak on main causeway to Angkor Wat

"We close May, the first." I couldn't believe it, what with all the beauty and the wonderful swimming, and it gave me an idea. "If I can get a group of my friends to come down on May the first, will you keep the hotel open? We can have a party on the roof of the pavilion for Decoration Day." André thought for a moment and then said, "*Mais oui,* I'll do it. But by the way, just who is Monsieur Day?"

I learned later that André had been an admirer of the United States Marines for a long time, and I have often wondered if the fact that I was a Marine had anything to do with his quick decision to go along with my idea.

I had a tough time selling my friends in Paris on Antibes. They all seemed to take the same attitude: "Who in hell goes south in the summertime?" Finally I was able to get together a group from Paris and London, and we left Paris for the south of France on the night of April 30, 1926. I had called André and suggested how he should assign quarters, and also to be sure to have sufficient transportation at the Antibes station.

Included in the group were Alexander Woollcott; Noel Coward; Sir Hugo "Sugie" de Bathe, married to Lily Langtry; Dwight Wiman and his wife, Steve; Cole Porter (Dwight and Cole had been schoolmates at Yale); Sir Montague Norman, governor of the Bank of England; Grace

Grace Moore aquaplaning off Eden Roc, 1926

Ernest Torrence, Bill Powell, Mrs. Torrence, Ronald Colman, Eden Roc, 1927

Moore; Beatrice Lillie; Gertrude Lawrence; Harpo Marx; and Dudley Field Malone, famed divorce lawyer in Paris. Within ten days, we were joined by Michael Arlen; Charles Brackett; the Sanford sisters, Gertrude and Janie; the Lengendre brothers, Morris and Sidney (Gertie Sanford and Sidney were later married); Charlie McArthur; and an amiable girl from England whose southern façade earned her the only name I can remember: the *Londonderrière*. Incidentally, the party on the roof of the pavilion for Decoration Day was an outstanding success. Among residents on the Côte d'Azur who attended were the Gerald Murphys, Scott Fitzgerald and his Zelda, Somerset Maugham, the Philip Barrys, and Mary Garden, who had retired from the opera and was living year-round in a house in the hills back of Monte Carlo.

With so many sun and fun lovers, it would have been difficult indeed not to have enjoyed one's self. The casino at Juan-les-Pins was open and became almost a nightly must. I once saw Jenny Dolly, one of the famous Dolly sisters, with her rich Belgian suitor beside her at the baccarat table, wager six million francs (the franc was thirty to the dollar) on the turn of a card, and win. Ofttimes residents of the Cap would return in the early morning hours for a skinny dip at Eden Roc. There were bullfights at Fréjus, horse races at Nice, and always for dinner the legendary Colombe d'Or restaurant in the mountains at Saint-Paul-de-Vence.

One of the most enjoyable things about the Riviera in 1926 was the lack of traffic. I can remember driving almost the entire length of the Croisette in Cannes without passing another car coming or going!

The following summer found the Cap fairly crowded, but still lots of fun. In 1928 and 1929, the only change was the more and more crowded condition, not only of Eden Roc but the entire Riviera. The American stock market collapse in the fall of 1929 caused little change in 1930, except that there were fewer Americans to be seen. The market crash didn't affect me too much, since my wherewithal came from the ground. In 1931, the crowds on the Riviera were unbelievable. I have long thought that, whenever any place becomes too crowded, especially with people you don't know, it is high time to leave, and I did. I haven't been back since.

The Hotel du Cap was the first important hotel on the French Riviera to stay open during summer months, and now it is open *only* in the summer. God bless André Sella, wherever he is.

During the five-year period from February 1927 through February 1932, I made trips on three completely divergent modes of transportation, in three different parts of the world.

The first was a trip down the ice-packed Cresta Run at Saint-Moritz, lying facedown on a steel contraption called a skeleton, with my face a mere eight inches above the ice. On the way down were two sharply banked curves, each some thirty feet high, and your speed at the bottom of the mile-long run was approximately eighty miles an hour. I didn't fool around. On my very first effort, I broke every existing record for elapsed time. That is to say, I doubt if any rider will ever take as long to negotiate the ride from the top.

The next trip was made the following year, 1928. After a three-month stay in Shanghai, I was bemoaning the fact that it took so long to get to France via steamship when I learned that the trip could be accomplished in half the time via the Trans-Siberian Railroad. A travel agent informed me that normally there was a weekly deluxe train from Vladivostok to Moscow but, at the time, it wasn't functioning. So I settled for a compartment in a first-class car on a regular train; not as fast as the deluxe, but still faster than a boat. When apprised of my decision, an American Club friend suggested that I purchase some rubles from Russian noblemen who had brought them out of Russia. Since the Communist takeover, rubles had become more and more worthless, except in Russia. Knowing that quite a few of the wealthier White Russians frequented Thurman Hyde's nightclub, the Del Monte, I hied myself to the Del Monte, told Thurman what I was trying to find, and he introduced me to several Russians. A purchase was consummated the next day at the American Club.

I can't remember just why I bought so many rubles as I did, most probably because they were so cheap. Later on, I was very glad I had. Neither can I remember how many thousands of rubles my $700 bought. Mind you, the $700 were Mexican dollars, each worth about a quarter as much as an American dollar so, actually, the rubles cost me less than $200 in U.S. currency.

Having been warned about taking rubles into Russia, I arrived in Vladivostok with a bulging money belt under my shirt. In the bar of the Metropole Hotel, I ran into an Englishman who had something to do with English–Russian relations and had made five trips on the Trans-Siberian, one of which was aboard a first-class train. Over several jolts of vodka, he enlightened me on what to expect. It was not encouraging. On the so-called first-class train, there was no dining car, and the coaches were old Wagonlit coaches of a vintage that were made before corridors. The compartments ran crosswise, with a door at either end, a built-in toilet on one side, and a washbasin on the other.

When I told him that I had booked an entire compartment, he said, "You'll be glad you did, because at every stop dozens and dozens of would-be travelers besiege the trains in an effort to go somewhere else. Be sure to keep your doors locked and the shades drawn every time the train stops." "What about food?" I asked. "There are certain stops designated as 'meal stops,' where you can fill yourself up with lousy cabbage soup, but as that necessitates leaving the train, I'd suggest that you take with you an ample supply of tinned goods, crackers, bottled water, and plenty of vodka, which, believe me, you'll need."

The Englishman was a real nice chap and proved it the next morning when he not only helped me round up provisions, but also helped me load the purchases into my compartment. As the supplies took up a lot of space in the compartment, I was more than glad that I was the sole occupant.

At noon, I was off and running; perhaps *jogging* would be a more descriptive word. I'd been told that at every late-afternoon stop, an attendant would climb aboard with fresh linen to arrange a makeshift bed and refill the washbasin tank. It was as simple as that. All in all, aside from the worn condition and the miniature toilet seat, the compartment was adequate—just.

On the station platform at Irkutsk, the first main stop west of Harbin, several women strolled along the cars with big trays on their heads, and each tray was loaded with small wooden platters of fresh, gray caviar taken from Lake Baikal sturgeon. Despite the fact that I had already eaten my fill of what could have been the forebears of the sturgeon roe, through the top half of the locked door I purchased three platters, each holding approximately a pound and a half. It was perfectly delicious caviar, and I ate it with a spoon.

During the first three days of the single-track trek, the train had stopped more than once in the middle of nowhere—no station, not a house to be seen anywhere.

Finally, at one of the unscheduled stops, I poked my head out and spotted a group of men squatted in a circle near the engine. Climbing out of the compartment, I sauntered toward the group to find out what it was all about. I found out: the train crew was having tea!

Some thirty-six hours after leaving Irkutsk, we came to Omsk on the River Irtysh, and again, there were women on the platform peddling caviar. And again, I bought three platters, which I spooned through the Ural Mountains for a day and a half before reaching Samara on the Volga River. Here, there were more women with trays of caviar, and this time, I went for four platters. As often happens when anyone becomes oversatiated with a particular edible, they are apt thereafter to add a *dis-* to the word *like* when discussing its merits. And that was exactly what happened to me. I have disliked caviar ever since. Incidentally, the fifteen pounds of caviar purchased with my cheap rubles cost me about as much as a cup of borscht would cost today at 21.

As I didn't want to leave Moscow with thousands of rubles still in my possession, I wondered again how I could spend them. A Cunard Line office near my hotel gave me an idea, so I dropped in with a question. "Can I buy a first-class ticket from Moscow, through Paris, to New York with rubles?" I asked. When the agent came back, "Most certainly, why not?" I dumped the rubles in my money belt on the counter. We counted them, to find that I not only had enough for a ticket from Moscow to New York and back to Paris but enough for two additional, open, roundtrip tickets from Paris to New York. Hallelujah! My inadvertent, over-extended purchase of rubles in Shanghai had bought six first-class transatlantic crossings for the horrendous sum of $30 each. I've often tried to remember just which of my Shanghai friends it was who suggested that I buy rubles. He deserved my sincere thanks.

My third uncommon trip occurred in February 1932, when I was one of twelve passengers aboard the *Graf Zeppelin* on its first transatlantic flight from Pernambuco,

Brazil, to Friedrichshafen, Germany. It was delightful. Captain Eckener charted his course so as to bypass air disturbances, thereby eliminating practically all vibration and feeling of motion. As the five motor gondolas were all aft of the passenger gondola, there was very little noise. The food was excellent, as was the service. True, the *Graf* wasn't as fast as modern-day jets, but still, it was twice as fast as the fastest ocean liner.

The night before we reached Gibraltar, Von Schiller, the *Graf*'s third officer, came up with an idea for a pool, the winner to be determined by the minute, of any hour, the nose of the dirigible reached an imaginary line extending due south from Gibraltar to the North African coast. All of the passengers put up five dollars, for which they drew five slips of paper from a hat. The slips were numbered from zero to sixty. On one of my slips was the number seventeen. So, the following morning when the touch time of 7:17 was sent down from the bridge, I had won what was probably the first air pool ever.

From Gibraltar, the *Graf* followed the Spanish Mediterranean coastline to Barcelona. It was a Sunday, and a bullfight was in progress. As we cruised slowly over the bullring, looking down at the thousands of upturned faces was a sight I'll long remember. Leaving Barcelona, the *Graf* set a northeasterly course that found us over the snow-covered, moonlit peaks of the Alps before midnight. And I might add, that too was quite a sight.

Approaching Friedrichshafen, the *Graf* was nosed down to no more than two or three hundred feet above the town, and we watched as all of its lights blinked an on-and-off welcome. In the early morning, handlines were dropped fore and aft, and the big bag pulled down to her home base. In the hangar, we were shown a miniature mock-up of the ill-fated *Hindenburg*.

There may be better ways to cover long distances from one place to another, but I can truthfully say that, in my fourteen globe-circling jaunts, I never found one comparable to the *Graf Zeppelin*.

There were playboys before 1920 and after 1940, but without doubt it was the era between those dates that was the heyday of playboys, and New York City the Mecca to which they flocked from everywhere. The noted columnist O.O. McIntyre once wrote, "A playboy is a wealthy, young man who likes to be where the lights are brightest and fun the most." And that is exactly what New York had to offer: bright lights and fun, plus an elegant sufficiency of what the statue in its harbor represents.

Heading the list of local and international playboys was one born in New York, on Fifth Avenue. His name—William Bateman Leeds, and he had every McIntyre requisite: plenty of money (his father had been one of the founders of American Can), youth, and an ever-present desire to enjoy himself. However, Bill Leeds didn't spend his money on himself only. He liked to do nice things for others less fortunate and, by his many kind acts, helped disprove the sometimes expressed theory that playboys were nothing more, or less, than wastrels.

Bill spread his largess far and wide. In 1927, while fishing in Tahitian waters, he noticed a small, barren island crowded with makeshift huts and was told the island was used to confine lepers. Feeling sorry for the plight of the lepers, he called on the governor of the islands and offered to build, equip, and maintain a colony for them on the main island of Tahiti. His offer was gratefully accepted, and a compound constructed near Papeete. What's more, Bill thoughtfully arranged for a 35mm movie projector, a screen, and a number of feature films to be sent to the colony, and thereafter periodically would send a supply of current films. Bill Leeds was like that!

Bill Leeds's acts of generosity were ofttimes unpremeditated. I remember one such act that I'll pass along as an example. One bitterly cold January evening, Bill and I were having a parting shot with Joe Moss in his Broadway nightclub, the Hollywood. The last show was over, and several befurred showgirls had traipsed past our table on their way home, or elsewhere, when a small girl in a thin-looking cloth coat passed. Bill looked at her and then asked Joe, "Doesn't she get cold in that coat?" When Joe replied that she probably did, Bill said, "Call her back." Shortly after the pretty little girl had joined us, Bill asked her point-blank, "Honey, don't you get cold in that coat?" "I do indeed, Mr. Leeds, but it's the only one I have," answered the girl. Excusing himself, Bill went to a phone. His call completed, he returned to the table, and shortly thereafter suggested that the three of us accompany him to his house for a nightcap. Don't forget, in those long-ago days, a nightcap was often used to toast the rising sun! We left the Hollywood for Bill's penthouse on Beekman Place.

In Bill's bar, we were still working on our first nightcaps when one of New York's leading furriers arrived, accompanied by a man carrying a big box. Proceeding to the library, the man lifted three mink coats from the box and displayed them on a long couch. On each coat was a plainly visible price tag, one marked $4,000; another, $5,000; and the third, $6,000. When alerted that all was in readiness, Bill led the girl into the library and, pointing to the coats, said, "Pick the one you like, Honey, it's yours." After giving Bill a big hug, the girl looked over the three coats closely and chose the one marked $4,000. Behind her back, the furrier shook his head quickly from side to side, as he nudged Bill and whispered to him that he had purposely changed the high and low price tags—so sure was he that the girl would pick the coat marked $6,000. Completely ignoring the furriers' whisper, Bill said to the girl, "If that's the coat you want, my pet, put it on." I couldn't quite figure if the furrier had pulled a fast one, the girl knew her mink, or she didn't want to appear greedy. I like to think it was the last.

I'm fairly certain that Bill never laid eyes on the little girl again, because the next day he left on an extended trip, and, while he was away, the girl put on her mink coat and took off for California. Incidentally, she did quite well in movies. I hope the coat, in some small way, contributed to her success.

The world would be a better place to live if there were more guys like Bill Leeds around.

In 1935, General Kilpatrick, president of Madison Square Garden, got the idea that Siamese boxers might build up the lagging interest in fisticuffs, so Dan Topping and I spent four months in the Orient trying to find Siamese boxers, with no success. We spent a month in Honolulu on our way home!

January 1938 found Jack "Shipwreck" Kelly, Bob Topping and me boarding the round-the-world cruise ship *Franconia* for a three-month African safari. After a stop in Rio, we left for Capetown via the island of St. Helena. When we anchored off Jamestown, the one port in St. Helena, most of the passengers left the ship for a visit to Longwood, the last "home" of Napoleon. The three of us went ashore around noon but, not finding much to look at in Jamestown, hired a car and drove up to the hills where Longwood is located. All of the passengers from the ship had left before we arrived, but a very nice caretaker showed us around. Several times he impressed on us that everything was exactly as Napoleon had left it: a shawl tossed over the back of a chair; a brandy snifter on a table; and three billiard balls and two pool cues on a billiard table. Nothing had been touched—until then.

We returned to Jamestown and boarded a launch out to the *Franconia*, which was due to up-anchor at five o'clock. We were sitting in the smoke room at 5:30, and the hook was still down. At six o'clock it was still down. Noticing several police boats milling around, I went on deck where the first officer was standing at the deck rail. "What's holding us up?" I asked him. "Someone stole one of Napoleon's balls," he answered, "and they won't clear us until it is returned." Standing at the rail, farther along the deck, I spotted Kelly. Walking up to him I held out my hand and said, "Give it to me." "How'd you know?" he questioned, as he placed a billiard ball in my hand. "Who else?" I replied.

I placed the ball on an ashtray in the deserted deck

Bill Leeds, 1937

lounge, telephoned the purser's office, and told them where it could be found. Within fifteen minutes, we were under way. Good Ole Kel later said that he had been thinking of dropping the ball over the side and was just about to do it. Thank God he hadn't—we might still be on St. Helena. After a three-month safari in British East Africa, we returned to the States the long way, across the Indian Ocean to Singapore and then on through Manila and Honolulu.

On August 18, 1938, Muriel Claffey and I were married on the flying bridge of Bill Leeds's yacht *Moana,* which was tied up at a Miami dock. Bill was best man and Olive, his wife, was matron of honor. A federal judge tied the knot. The ceremony was so short, it caused Olive to say, "For that, you could have skipped it." Following a reception-farewell party on the quarterdeck, the *Moana* cast off for an extended trip through the South Pacific.

Bill Leeds and the author, Bali, 1940

The *Moana* was a cute little craft of some two thousand tons and carried a crew of fifty-four, including a doctor and a registered nurse. It had an elevator and a swimming pool. Bill Leeds was a host par excellence, and, aboard the *Moana*, he more than lived up to his oft-expressed belief: "If a man doesn't know how to run a yacht, he doesn't deserve to own one." He maintained three shifts of chefs and three shifts of stewards, making it possible for his guests to order a dinner from soup to nuts at three in the afternoon or three in the morning, if that was what they wanted.

From the Pacific end of the Panama Canal, we headed west for Cocos Island, where we found the fishing even better than we'd been told it would be. Even Muriel boated three or four fairly large tuna, and she was not exactly what might be called a fisherwoman. Next, to the Galapagos Islands for more fishing. From there, we carried on westward to Tahiti. We were in Tahiti or Tahitian waters for nearly three months and enjoyed every minute. Often, I fished with Charles Nordhoff, author of *Mutiny on the Bounty*.

Charlie and I spent weeks fishing for marlin, without a single strike. But we didn't care. The air was warm, and the waters were blue. While fishing one day, Charlie asked me if I knew of a remedy for impetigo. Remedy? I didn't even know what impetigo was. But I asked the doctor aboard the *Moana* about it, and he gave me a fairly large bottle of gentian violet crystals. Besides being used in treating impetigo, gentian violet is a dye that requires maybe a dozen crystals to a gallon of water. The following day I gave Charlie the bottle of crystals. That evening I dined with him at his house, and I remember we were in the middle of an argument about the relative merits of Black Label versus White Label scotch when Charlie suddenly remembered the gentian violet. A small tin washtub was filled with water, and the entire bottle of crystals was dumped into it. Charlie then led out a sleepy, toddling case of impetigo— his fourteen-month-old daughter. Each of us held a wrist as we dunked her up and down in the tub of dye. I had violet spots on my hands for weeks!

Some months later I met a chap in Palm Springs who had recently returned from Tahiti, and I listened as he told a dinner-party about a little violet-colored girl he had seen on the streets of Papeete.

Bill Leeds and the author, Kuta Beach, Bali, 1940

Back in those days, the most popular late spot in Papeete was a thatched-roof nightclub called the Lafayette, where natives and visitors whooped and hollered all night. It seems that, in every French possession, there is always a Lafayette something-or-other. In Saigon, for instance, the Lafayette something-or-other was a house where women lived and men visited.

Chartering a course northward, the *Moana* touched at the islands of Bora-Bora, Fanning, and Palmyra before arriving in Honolulu for Christmas and a month's layover. Between Fanning and Palmyra, we ran into some high seas and the captain thought it best if we heaved to in the lee of an uninhabited island. Anchored there was a thirty-foot schooner that looked as though she had seen some rough going. A man rowed over from the schooner to ask if we could spare some line as most of his had been broken or carried away. He was asked aboard, and told us of the terrible weather he had encountered all the way from Wilmington harbor in California. He was an Englishman who had owned a small ranch in California. Deciding to look for greener pastures in New Zealand, he had sold his ranch, bought the schooner, and, with his family, was on his way "down under." His crew consisted of himself and one other man. His wife did the cooking and their two children did what they could to help. Bill invited them all to dinner.

During the evening, when told that the *Moana* carried a radiophone capable of reaching England, the Englishman seemed skeptical. Bill suggested he call some relative there and see for himself. The only relative he had left in England, it seemed, was an old aunt in Nottingham who probably thought that he was dead. "We'll call her," Bill said and ordered the call placed. When the connection was made, Bill and I accompanied the Englishman to the radio shack. He started off, "Aunt Jane, this is Edgar." There was a pause before a quavering voice said: "Who?" He repeated his name, whereupon Aunt Jane asked, "Edgar, where in the world *are* you?" "In the middle of the Pacific Ocean, Aunt Jane," answered Edgar. There was another silence, then a sort of bleated, "Oh, my God!" and that was all.

Our stay in Honolulu, where we tied up to a dock directly below the Aloha Tower, was truly delightful. Most of our daylight hours were spent either surfboarding, body surfing, or spending the day with Cris Holmes on his Coconut Island. One day there was an outrigger race off Waikiki Beach, with contestants vying for a silver cup presented by Bill. Following a two-day stop to try boating black marlin off Kona Point on the big island, Hawaii, the *Moana* headed east toward the California coast. Once there, she was tied up in San Diego harbor for six weeks, while we spent a month at Eddie Goulding's house in Palm Springs and two weeks in Beverly Hills.

We left San Diego for Acapulco with two additional guests on the passenger list, Joan Bennett and Woolworth Donahue. After watching the boys dive from the rocks in Acapulco, we drove up to Mexico City with an overnight stop in Taxco. Ten days later, having seen most everything there was to see in Mexico City, Joan and "Wooly" flew back to California and the rest of us drove back to Acapulco. Then it was back through the Panama Canal and on to Havana. It was nice getting back into home waters, but we most certainly left a lot of fun in the Pacific.

Before I knock off recounting some of my adventures between World War I and World War II, in case some of you might be wondering just how I could have afforded to lead

Cockfight, Tahiti, 1938

Cris Holmes and Duke Kahanamuku, Waikiki, 1939

the life I did, although it's none of your damn business, I'll tell you.

When I reached my majority, I inherited a 4,200-acre plantation in eastern North Carolina, nearly half of which was covered by one of the largest tracts of virgin longleaf pine left in the state. A small town and a railway station were on the property, and a main highway bisected it. Half of the tillable soil was tended by sharecroppers, the other half by an overseer who planted and garnered cotton, corn, peanuts, and tobacco. If I tell you that I hardly knew the difference between a boll of cotton and an ear of corn, you can easily understand why I did not move to the plantation with the idea of operating it. The annual income from the plantation was ample to provide a comfortable living for anyone except a between-wars Marine with eyes on faraway places and a desire to shoot and fish. I therefore augmented my income by selling some of the pine trees. Whenever ready funds were getting low, I'd wire my attorney to sell some more trees.

There were many coveys of quail on the plantation, and I had three damned good bird dogs to find them. Every year, when I could fit the time in, I'd go down for a couple of weeks to shoot quail. Egon turned into one of the best retrievers I've ever seen. He would watch a dead bird go down and often would find the dead bird before the bird dogs. He'd bring me the bird, place it in my hand, sit down, and raise a paw to be congratulated. The other dogs thought he was some kind of nut.

Anyway, regardless of what I did, or how I did it, nobody—I repeat, nobody—ever had a better time spending an inheritance.

About a year and a half before Americans became entangled in the second "war to end all wars," I heard that on a New York dock were fifteen Chevrolet chassis that had been donated to the American Field Service and were slated for Holland. The Germans had just overrun the Netherlands, so the chassis had nowhere to go. To rectify such a situation, I became embroiled in a war America hadn't even entered. If I hadn't been the sort of Marine who looked for trouble, I doubt if I'd have gotten involved. Anyway, I discussed with Bill Leeds the possibility of securing the chassis, placing ambulance bodies on them, and taking them to Kenya as an American Field Service unit. Bill, who liked to do anything unusual, thought the idea great. I then went to Steven Galatti, head man of the American Field Service, and explained my idea to him. Galatti thought the idea sound, but said we'd first have to get an acceptance from the Kenya government. I told Galatti that, in 1938, while on a safari, I had met and dined at Government House with Sir Philip Mitchell, the governor of Kenya, and I wondered if it might be some kind of an "in." He said, "Fine! Let's get a cable off to the governor." Two days later, a cable from Sir Philip stated that an American Field Service unit would be more than gladly accepted and suggested that the ambulance bodies be put on in Nairobi.

Toward the end of August, the chassis, along with two mechanics, fifty spare tires, and a large supply of spare parts, were loaded on a Robin Line ship bound for Mombasa, Kenya. Bill covered the cost of the junket, but it hardly made a dent in his American Can fortune. As plane travel from the United States to Africa was practically nonexistent, Bill and I had decided to get to Africa the long way via San Francisco, a Pan Am Clipper to Manila, and a Dutch passenger freighter across the Indian Ocean via the Island of Maritius to Mombasa. Bill and I, along with three other passengers, completed the passenger list aboard the *Stratts Malakka.*

When the *Stratts* dropped her hook in the harbor of Maritius, an emissary from Government House came aboard with an invitation for Bill and me to lunch with the governor, Sir Bede Clifford, who had previously been the governor of Nassau, and both of us knew him. Proving how strange things have a way of happening: also at the luncheon was the skipper of an English cruiser anchored in the harbor. Bill and the skipper had been schoolmates at Eton!

About halfway between Maritius and Mombasa, the captain of the *Stratts Malakka* received a radio message stating that a German submarine had been sighted off Mombasa, so he headed southwest to Durban.

In Durban, I rushed ashore to try and find out how we could get to Mombasa. Fortunately, there was a South African troopship leaving for Mombasa the following midnight, and we angled a ride. The commanding officer of troops aboard the troopship for some reason resented the fact that two Americans had been allowed passage and did everything he could to make our lives miserable. He even had us assigned bunks in the bowels of the ship. There was one really nice chap aboard, a Major Durston, who was headed north with his squadron to drop bombs on the Eyeties. He helped Bill and me deplete the supply of booze in the ship's smokeroom.

Shortly after we docked in Mombasa, Sir Philip Mitchell, who happened to be in Mombasa, came aboard to welcome the heads of the American Field Service unit, and Bill and I more or less got even with the obnoxious commanding officer when the governor practically bypassed him to greet us. The look on his face seemed to say, "What have I done?" Sir Philip told us that the chassis had arrived in Nairobi two days before and gave us the name of the best firm to attach the ambulance bodies. He also asked us to accompany him in his private railway car for the overnight ride to Nairobi, which we did, and we found the "Guv" to be a more than congenial host.

Ensconced in the New Stanley Hotel, we started making plans to have ambulance bodies attached to the chassis. With the chassis had been shipped a Chevrolet sedan, so transportation was no problem. I still have my British East Africa driving permit.

On a visit to the governor, we were told that the ambulance unit would be attached to the King's African Rifles, and drivers had been secured from their ranks. When the bodies were in place and a truck had been provided to transport the mechanics, tires, and spare parts, we headed north to the Tana River, the so-called front in the Northern Frontier district of Kenya.

It took less than a month to realize that there were more ambulances than there were wounded, so we turned the ambulances over to the King's African Rifles and returned to Nairobi. To assuage the governor for our "pull-out," Bill gave the city of Nairobi a serviceman's club.

I may have been wrong, but it appeared to me that the British-Italian fracas in Kenya smacked of the sort of war in which neither side particularly cared what went on. The South Africans were a long way from home, and so were the Italians. A South African bomber pilot took off from Malindi, a coast town north of Mombasa, with a planeload of bombs to be dropped on Italian Somaliland, some five hundred miles to the northeast. When no more than ten miles north of the Kenya border, he dropped the bombs on a cornfield and returned to Malindi. He immediately became known as the Kernel. A former white hunter, who dropped an Italian fighter plane with a single rifle shot; thereafter he was called the Ace. The last two stories typified the feel of the war.

Bill and I ran into a real problem when we tried to get out of Africa. The war in Europe had raised hob with all kinds of transportation. Bill cabled Lord Mountbatten in London, and I cabled "Ribbs" McAdoo in New York, who was president of a round-the-world steamship line. A return cable from McAdoo advised us that we had space in a ship leaving Capetown for New York four days hence. And then, by God! we couldn't get space in a plane to Capetown. Finally, we were able to secure space in a ship out of Mombasa to Singapore via the Seychelle Islands and Colombo. The mechanics returned with us.

In Singapore we again hit a snag. We couldn't get to Manila. Three weeks later we were fortunate in securing passage in a Japanese ship, the *Tatsutu Maru*, due to sail one midnight. As Bill had been imbibing more than a bit, I instructed the two mechanics, Raffi and Harry, to get him aboard by ten o'clock. I watched as Bill, in a white suit, was helped through the Raffles Hotel lobby by Raffi and Harry. I arrived at the ship around eleven and was greeted at the head of the gangway by a very excited Raffi. "Where is Mr. Leeds?" I asked. "I don't know, Mr. Finney. I left him in his cabin when I went to get something to eat and when I got back he wasn't there!" Just then, a military vehicle drove onto the dock and pulled up at the foot of the gangway. Two British soldiers helped out of the car the damndest-looking ball of black mud and pushed it up the gangway. It was Bill.

Apparently Bill had wandered down the gangway, across the dock, and fallen into the shallow, black ooze on the other side. He had struggled through the muck to shore. There a sentry had challenged him and then gone through his pockets for some kind of identification. All he could find was a slip of paper with "Leeds, Raffles Hotel" thereon. The sentry called Raffles, to be told that Mr. Leeds had checked out and was sailing in the *Tatsutu Maru* at midnight. Bill was taken below, washed thoroughly, and put to bed.

The *Tatsutu* was filled with Japanese men who had obviously been called back to their homeland for a reason, but I'll have to admit that the four Americans aboard were given the best of service.

The first available Clipper left Manila for the States eight days after our arrival. While awaiting our departure, Bill started nipping again and kept a tight grip on a bottle through our overnight stops at Guam, Wake, and Midway.

As a sidelight to the proficiency of Pan Am navigators, I relate a story that happened on our second day out of Manila. Since leaving Guam, we had flown over a cloud strata and hadn't been able to see the ocean below us even once. As the plane approached Wake Island, the captain, Steve Bancroft, an old friend of mine from tuna tournament days at Cat Cay, sent word asking me to come on the bridge. As Steve nosed the plane down for the landing at Wake, I watched the altimeter drop from 1,000 feet to 900 feet, and to 800 feet just as we entered the cloud strata. Not having been able to see anything but sky and the top of the strata all day, I asked Steve, "Suppose when we break through this stuff there's no Wake Island?" "We're in one hell of a fix," answered Steve, " 'cause that's where it is supposed to be." We broke into the clear at about 200 feet and there, directly in front of us, was the landing lagoon at Wake! Steve hardly had to touch the steering wheel to make a perfect landing.

As our wives were meeting us in California, I deemed it wise to leave the plane in Honolulu and carry on to the West Coast by surface craft, which would allow Bill ten days or so to dry out. And that's what we did. After four days at the Royal Hawaiian, we boarded the *Lurline* and were on our last leg back to the States. Bill took his drying out period seriously and, as a result, walked down the gangway at San Pedro looking like a new man. Muriel and Olive were on the dock to greet us.

Thus ended a sincere effort to help somebody. Our effort must have been appreciated, as we were both awarded the George and African Star medals by Great Britain.

7 | World War II–
South Pacific

ON DECEMBER 7, 1941, I WAS SITTING WITH DAN TOPPING, Grantland Rice, and Bill Corum in the Polo Grounds, watching the Brooklyn Dodger football team defeat the Giants in the last game of the season. At the end of the first half, "Granny" left the box to visit the sportswriter's booth. Shortly, he returned. "I have just heard the damndest thing," he said. "The Japs have invaded Pearl Harbor!" *Invaded* turned out to be the wrong word, since the only

Japs to land on Hawaii were dead bomber pilots. Anyway, *invaded* or whatever, the story, if true, definitely presaged the entry of the United States into World War II. When the game ended, the four of us headed for the Dodger dressing room. Word of Pearl Harbor must have just reached the players. As we entered, one of the players was standing on a table shouting, "What th' hell, if we can beat the Giants, we damn well can beat the Japs. Bring 'em on!"

That night, I was kept awake wondering if I could again wear the globe and anchor. However, my ardor cooled a bit by morning, when I gave more thought to my disability discharge and approaching forty-second birthday. I drifted worriedly along on the surf and bubble of life's current for about three months, until I started noticing Marines of my age in uniform. Then I started wondering again. I have to thank Put Humphries, one of the nicer guys around town, for providing the clincher.

Put called one morning to ask if I could lunch with him; he had something he wanted me to see. When I arrived at 21 there was Put, all done up in a brand-new Navy officer's uniform. Just that morning, he had received his commission as a naval lieutenant, along with orders to report to Pensacola for flight training. After lunch, I headed to Dunhill's to pick up some tobacco. Put decided he needed some tobacco too, so he came along. As we were about halfway down the block on Fifth Avenue, two British sailors, headed uptown, came to sharp salutes and held them as we passed. Put did nothing! "Put," I said, "those sailors saluted. Why didn't you return their salute?" "Damn!" Put came back, "were they in our Navy?"

Right then, I began thinking that if the military was taking on officers who didn't even have an inkling about military etiquette, there must be a chance for me. That afternoon, I wrote a letter requesting a commission in the Marine Corps and mailed it special delivery. Within a week, I received a reply from Marine Headquarters informing me that, before I could be considered for a commission, I would have to procure a waiver from the Bureau of Surgery. I flew to Washington the next morning for a visit to the bureau. Without much ado, I wangled a waiver and then hied myself to Marine Headquarters on Constitution Avenue, where I filled out a formal application for a commission and attached my waiver thereto.

As six weeks went by without even as much as a postcard from Constitution Avenue, I couldn't help but get the impression that possibly the Marine Corps wasn't too anxious to take on a formerly disabled, forty-two-year-old retread. As much as I hated to, I began thinking about other branches of the military.

A friend of mine, Commander John Bergen, was in Washington on the Secretary of the Navy's staff, and I called Jack to ask if he could arrange an appointment for me to see someone of importance in Naval Intelligence. I roughly recounted my military past and my linguistic abilities. When I told him that I spoke Swahili, Jack came back, "Swahili. What in hell is that?" He has called me Swahili ever since. An appointment was made.

Jack's office was in the same building as Marine Headquarters. At the entrance, I was met by a young Navy lieutenant who escorted me to Jack's office. His name was Alfred Vanderbilt! I can't remember if Admiral Towers was the head man in Naval Intelligence or not, but it was to his upstairs office that Jack took me. Shortly after the admiral's interrogation had started, a Marine colonel came in the room and sat down. It was Colonel John Thomason, of World War I fame in France. He was in the throes of formulating a Marine Intelligence unit of its own, something they'd never had before. During the interview, when I mentioned to Admiral Towers the fact that I had seen action with the Fifth Regiment in France, Colonel Thomason broke in, "Did you say you saw action with the Fifth Regiment?" "Yes sir, I did. I was in Captain Lem Shepherd's company in the first battalion," I answered. "Then why are you trying to join the 'swab-jockeys'?" the colonel asked.

Because, sir, I have a feeling that I'm being pushed around trying to get back in the Corps," I replied. "Don't you sign a thing until you hear from me," the colonel said. End of interview.

Within two weeks, my commission as a first lieutenant came through, with orders to report to Quantico for a "refresher" course.

I spent the day before I was due to report in Washington, with the idea of trying to talk to Colonel Jerry Jerome, in charge of officer assignments, about skipping the refresher course. I was able to see Colonel Jerome mainly, I'm sure, because I was a World War I Marine. I told him that I had not forgotten one thing I had been taught at Parris Island, and had traveled extensively through the islands of the Pacific. Because of the rumor that Marines would shortly be sent to New Caledonia, I stressed the point that I spoke French, something that might be helpful. My French was anything but Parisian. It was a sort of patois that I'd already found bore a resemblance to the French spoken on French-speaking islands in the Pacific. I must have talked pretty good, because the colonel finally said, "You go on down to Quantico and report. You'll hear from me soon."

In Quantico, I was being readied to be "refreshed" when I received a dispatch from Washington ordering me to report as intelligence officer to the Twenty-fifth Marine Air Group at Coronado, California, for duty overseas. In the barracks near an open window, I was packing my gear and couldn't help but hear the commanding officer tell the "refresher" boys, lined up in formation, "Don't any of the rest of you get the idea that you'll be receiving a dispatch from Washington. Lieutenant Finney's was the last."

I reported to Colonel P. K. Smith at the Twenty-fifth Marine Air Group. When I hesitatingly asked him the duties of an intelligence officer, he thought mightily for a moment and then answered, "Hell! You're the intelligence officer. You figure it out." Taking the colonel at his word, all I could do was my best. I even made two parachute jumps at nearby

Matthews Field. Just why, I'll never know. But then, I came up with something that I knew always sits well with Marines. Or should I say, "Sips well?"—in other words, an antidote for snakebite. Liquor was hard to get, but I got it, over a hundred cases, and eight hundred cases of Shasta Beer. Although knowing it was a lie, I had to convince several distributors that poisonous snakes abounded on many islands in the Pacific. They didn't know, so what the hell! Purchasing the liquor posed no problem, since the supply officer agreed with me that the welfare of the troops should be a top priority. I had the whole lot packed in wooden crates marked "Aviation Supplies," with a code name on each denoting its contents.

Shove-off time arrived, and all officers were told to be aboard the *President Monroe* by midnight for an early morning departure. Three of us were assigned to a single cabin in which the beds had been replaced by two double-decker bunks. I grabbed one of the lower bunks. Sometime during the night, I was vaguely aware that a fourth occupant had entered the cabin, stashed his gear, and climbed into the empty bunk above mine. Shortly after daylight, I was awakened by a face peering down on me and a voice saying, "Well, I'll be damned!" The face and voice belonged to Jeff Downey, my pup-tent buddy from Parris Island, who had occupied the bunk above mine in the *Henderson* on our way to France. We hadn't seen each other since he was wounded at Saint-Mihiel. He told me what had happened. The headquarter's company of an engineering battalion had been misloaded on the *Monroe* instead of the *Malolo,* which was docked just ahead of us and slated to sail in the same convoy. Jeff and I had a great time swapping lies all the way to Noumea, but unfortunately it turned out to be our last trip together. I helped bury Jeff on Guadalcanal.

After the *Monroe* had tied up in Noumea, the native dock wallopers must have had to wonder at just how many planes were being flown in to deliver such a massive amount of "aviation supplies." It didn't take too much doing to convince Colonel "P.K." that it might be wise if I remained in Noumea to supervise the unloading of the supplies. I also suggested that he assign a squad of men to ride herd on them to make sure they arrived safely at Tontuta Airfield, some twenty miles to the west, where the group was to be stationed. I held out a couple of crates of liquor—crates, mind you, not cases—and 100 cases of beer, to be delivered to Wing Headquarters at Cheberta on the outskirts of Noumea. This decision came under the heading of quick thinking, as I had already decided that I'd rather be in town than in the country. I told Colonel "P.K." that they had been lost in the shuffle. However, some days later, while he was lunching at headquarters mess, I couldn't help but notice that, when he was offered a bottle of Shasta beer, he gave me a quizzical look.

When I had first suggested that I remain in Noumea to oversee the unloading of the supplies, I hadn't known of the lack of living space. After several tries, I ended up at the Sevastopol Hotel, a small hotel in the center of town, where I was told their only vacant room was reserved for an Army colonel. Fortunately I learned that the owner was originally from Juan-les-Pins on the French Riviera, a spot I knew well. It was then that my knowledge of French patois first came in handy. Over a few nips, the owner and I talked at length about the wonders of the Riviera from Toulouse to Ventimiglia. When the late-arriving colonel finally arrived, he was informed that his tardiness had caused a cancellation of his reservation. The owner asked me to interpret the diatribe the colonel was delivering because he did not have a room. In my translation, I managed to slip in a few aspersions concerning the owner's ancestry. Incensed, the owner screamed at the colonel to get the hell out—and I got his room.

The owner and I became bosom buddies, and I kept the room during my entire sixteen months in and out of Noumea, at a cost of six cartons of American cigarettes per month! Ofttimes I'd let friends use the room. One, I remember, was Gene Markey, on a trip up from New Zealand. Gene was formerly married to Joan Bennett, the youngest of the three glamorous Bennett sisters. I also remember that Gene never got over the beautiful French gal that lived in the next room at the Sevastopol, nor would he believe that she was married, or that I never saw her but once, maybe twice.

On board the *Monroe* had been several staff officers on their way to join General Roy Geiger, commanding general of the First Marine Air Wing. Hearing about my farsightedness in arranging for the group's extra aviation supplies, the general figured that such talent should be transferred to the parent outfit, the First Wing. So I was moved from a job I knew little about to a job I knew nothing about. My dilemma was soon solved, however, when a dispatch arrived from Guadalcanal ordering a ground installation officer to be flown up. Not that I knew what a ground installation job was either, but ace fighter pilot Joe Foss will tell you that I filled the bill, directing a squad of men in digging bomb shelters into which ground personnel could crawl when the Tokyo Express made its daily bombing raid.

The day I arrived on the Canal, I was on my way to report to Colonel Bauer in a tent just off the fighter strip, when I noticed a small howitzer battery that had been lined up on a slight rise at the west end of the strip. I watched as the battery fired a salvo across the Tenaru River, two miles or so to the east. Then it turned around and fired a salvo across the Lunga River, a mile or so to the west! Bloody Ridge, which was Jap country, was located between the Lunga and the Tenaru no more than two miles south of the beach. Once I realized this, it became fairly obvious that the Marines occupied a very small beachhead, roughly an area the size of Central Park, and were in a somewhat cramped position.

That night all hell broke loose. A Jap battlewagon, two or three cruisers, and a flock of destroyers lay offshore and shelled us all night. To add to the confusion, overhead bombers joined in. As I lay in a shellhole shaking the ground

Guadalcanal wasn't too uncomfortable, 1942

around me every bit as much as the Jap shells, all I could think about was why I hadn't listened more closely to my cousin's second admonition, the one about keeping my mouth shut. If I had, I would have still been in Quantico instead of being scared to death on Guadalcanal. I'd like to add here that any man who says he isn't scared when he's under shellfire is a damned liar. Our ammunition dump was completely demolished. The Japs didn't know it, but the next day we had hardly enough ammo left to arm the five planes that hadn't been hit. The damaged planes were propped up in line to look operational to Jap observers in the hills, and, when the Tokyo Express came down the slot, they were met by our five planes just as though there were plenty more where they came from.

As supply ships were few and far between, food on the island was not only scarce but God-awful. For a while, the basic ingredient of nearly every meal was maggoty rice, which had been left behind by the Japs, with an occasional bit of Spam. In no time at all, I realized that going to France from Parris Island had been practically a pleasure when

Lowell Reeves, the author, and Joe Foss, Guadalcanal, 1942

compared with coming to Guadalcanal from El Morocco. However, some edibles weren't too bad. For instance, the ripe coconuts were both tasty and plentiful.

The Japs had dragged a three-inch naval gun through the jungle and backed it into a cave, to keep our planes from spotting its location. Because of its depth in the cave, it could not be aimed at the north end of Henderson Field, where our transport planes were unloaded. But it could zero in on the middle of both Henderson Field and the fighter strip. We called the gun Millimeter Mike. Every now and then, when there were no planes overhead, Mike would let go at any movement on either strip.

One day while I was enjoying a coconut in front of my tent, a major from Marine Headquarters, Washington, who had just arrived for his first trip to Cactus, the code name for Guadalcanal, stopped by and asked if I could direct him to the Operations tent of the fighter squadrons. As it was directly across the fighter strip from my tent and I was headed that way, I told him that I'd show him. We were walking across the strip when BAM! I heard Mike let one go. "Hit the deck," I hollered, and we did. The shot was short. As we scrambled to our feet and started running to the safety of the coconut trees, the major inquired, "How the hell did you get

In back of the ready tent, Guadalcanal, 1942

under me?" "A little trick I learned in World War I," I replied. And that was only one trick.

Things went on in the Solomons that never would have been allowed in either Central Park or on a plane to Washington. Whenever a Jap sniper was spotted high in a coconut tree, the boys would grab their rifles and wager who would be the first to shoot him out of the tree. As two Japs, who understood English, were being flown down from Rendova to the Canal to be interrogated, their accompanying guard conferred with a member of the plane crew. As the plane neared the Russell Islands, the guard whispered to the Japs and told them, if they wanted to bail out, to grab the two parachutes on the floor near the door, quickly put them on, open the door—and jump. The Japs did just that. What the guard had failed to tell them was that those particular chutes were being flown down to Cactus to ascertain why they wouldn't open!

On clear nights, the Japs would send down from Kahili a slow, high-flying, single-engine plane that sounded not unlike a washing machine. It would wheel overhead, drop a stick of small bombs, and go home. We called the plane Maytag Charlie and soon learned we did not have to worry unless Charlie was directly above. Actually it was more of a nuisance than anything else. Dropping the word that General Geiger was thinking of moving into our camp area, I had my squad of helpers construct a fairly large dugout covered with coconut logs between the tent I shared with three buddies and one erected, presumably, for the general with an entrance down into the dugout. As it so happened, at the other end of the dugout was an entrance into our tent. Quite a coincidence!

The former Japanese headquarters building had been converted into a field hospital. Unfortunately, a bomb had completely demolished it. On the afternoon of the day this had happened, returning after "washing" some clothes in the dirty water of the Lunga, I noticed in the rubble of the hospital an unscathed Japanese, kerosene-operated refrigerator. As a couple of my boys were in the truck with me, we stopped and loaded the icebox in the truck. Mentioning that it would be a convenience for General Geiger, I had it installed in a hole dug in one side of the dugout. In our tent, it might have caused questions.

Joe Foss, Duke Davis, and I were heavy sleepers, but the fourth man in our tent, Soupy Campbell, could hear the grass grow. He made a wonderful alarm clock and would awaken us only when he thought it really necessary. When he did, we would file down the narrow entrance into the dugout and wait for something to happen.

When Soupy was evacuated with a Jap bullet in his arm, he was replaced by Beanie Payne. Beanie was not only a heavy sleeper, he snored so loudly we could barely hear Maytag Charlie until he was directly overhead. A falling stick of bombs makes a distinct sound, and one night we all heard this sound at the same time. And we all made it to the dugout entrance at the same time—just before the bombs burst nearby. I'll let you guess which one of us broke through the jam and got into the dugout first. You're right—I did.

It rained so hard one morning that it seemed impossible for the fighter planes to take off through the mud and prevent the Jap bombers from coming in low on their daily bombing run. Joe Foss asked Colonel Bauer if he could give it a try. Joe argued that if he could get his plane in the air, so could the rest of the squadron. With an okay, Joe's plane was pushed and pulled as far back in the coconuts as it could be and held fast as Joe revved his motor. At a signal, all hands pushed instead of pulled, and Joe's plane splashed down the airstrip. Once Joe's plane was airborne, the other pilots climbed in their planes and followed. Incidentally, Joe Foss shot down three Jap bombers that day.

By no means have I meant to imply that Guadalcanal was the only tough spot in the Pacific, because there were many: Tarawa, Iwo Jima, Saipan, and Peleliu, to mention a few. The conquest of the Canal took longer mainly because the

The author and Joe Foss, Sydney, 1942

Japs were determined to use it as a stepping stone in their hoped-for capture of Australia.

Guadalcanal, Tarawa, Iwo Jima, Saipan, and Peleliu were all publicized as having been tough and rugged, and they were, but the capture of the island of Peleliu could have been the toughest. It didn't take long, but the Japs did their best to hold it, and the Marines lost a lot of personnel. Actually, there were 6,526 casualties on Peleliu, nearly as many as the combined casualties on Guadalcanal and Iwo Jima.

In mid-November 1942, Joe Foss and I were evacuated in the same transport plane. Both of us had bad cases of malaria and ended up in the Aviatorium, a residence near Cheberta that had been turned into a hospital. While there, we wangled two weeks' sick leave in Sydney, Australia. As the Marines were credited with having had a lot to do with stopping the Japanese offensive aimed at that country, Marines were welcomed to Sydney with open arms. Joe and I were among the first to be so welcomed. With his bag of twenty-two Jap zeros to date, Joe was automatically a hero. I was just another Marine. Food was rationed in Sydney, but when we visited Romano's, a restaurant directly across the street from our hotel, the maître-d'hôtel turned out to be Tony, whom I had known at Quaglino's in London. Tony was so glad to see someone he had known before, he told us to forget the ten-shilling limit on restaurant dining and to order anything we liked. He even went so far as to break out a couple of bottles of excellent champagne. Joe and I lunched and dined at Romano's practically every day, a far cry from the dry fish heads and maggoty rice we'd been getting on Guadalcanal.

The Australia Hotel bar was a favorite gathering place for Aussie officers. One day, while bellied up to the bar, I told a group of our newfound acquaintances a story that had just started making the rounds before I left the States. Two sharks, who usually swam around together, were separated during a bad storm in the English Channel. After searching for each other for weeks they finally got together again, but one was very fat and the other very thin. The thin shark cased the fat one and allowed, "You must have been eating pretty good." "Yeah," replied the fat shark, "I found a big fat Nazi and ate hell out of him. But what about you? You don't look like you've had a decent meal since I saw you last." "And I haven't," came back the thin shark. "But what really burned me up was that, just yesterday, I ran across a good-sized British sailor, ripped his uniform off and was about to eat him when I read, tattooed across his chest, 'There'll always be an England.' And you just can't swallow that crap." The Aussies loved that story, and from then on, I was known as The Shark Man to Joe's The Zero Chap.

Actually, it was because of the shark story that I ran into a classmate of mine from Virginia who was the naval officer in charge of Lend-Lease throughout Australia. I never understood just how Lend-Lease worked, but when my friend told me that the Marines on Guadalcanal rated anything they needed, I didn't give him an argument. It was through Lend-Lease that I was able to obtain a planeload of what I called necessities, including $500 worth of Christmas ornaments, tinned plum puddings, and twenty cases of Christmas cheer. Best of all, I managed to get the whole shemozzle to the Canal before Santa was due.

Just after Christmas, the Wing headquarters were moved from Guadalcanal to Espíritu Santo in the New Hebrides Islands, about halfway between the Canal and New Caledonia. As a ground installation officer wasn't needed on Espíritu, I was given a new title: "Wing Morale Officer." At least, I had a vague idea of what that was. With a little maneuvering, I was able to take over the Chaplain's "hut" when he moved into larger quarters. The hut comprised three smallish, collapsible huts rigged together in a row. I let my sergeant establish his office in the first, with my office in the middle and my cot in the third. Alongside the hut was a kind of shack made from split coconut trees, a square affair with one door its only entrance. It proved just the right spot to put a kerosene stove salvaged from a cracked-up PBY. If you wonder why a stove: it came in handy to cook, among other things, wild pigeons, which were plentiful on the island.

There have been many stories told about those hectic days on Guadalcanal, but I doubt if you've heard this one. In February 1943, a flattop dropped her hook in Bougainville Channel and on board was a print of the just-completed movie *Wake Island*. When someone suggested that *Wake Island* would be a natural first picture to be shown on the Canal, I went along with the idea and was able to trade a boatload of hearts of palm for use of the print, a projector, and a screen. These, my sergeant and I hauled with us on my next trip north.

On the Canal, I tented with an old friend Muggs Riley, commanding officer of the First Aviation Engineers, an outfit that was mainly responsible for keeping the airstrips operative. I decided that his command should have first crack at seeing *Wake Island*. Muggs's outfit was encamped in a muddy area near Henderson Field. Word of the first movie on Guadalcanal must have spread like wildfire as darkness found the small, open area in which the screen had been rigged on the rear of a truck literally crawling with gyrenes. Every tree was loaded after all space in the mud had been taken. The projector had been set up in another truck and connected to a portable generator. Not many remembered Maytag Charlie or the Tokyo Express, but they had certainly been told.

The picture was running smoothly enough until bombs started falling on Wake Island. Then all hell broke loose. Guys jumped out of trees to look for cover; the generator was stopped and complete silence reigned. But there were no Jap bombs—no nothing! When the generator was started again and the light from the projector thrown on the area not a man was to be seen. All hands had mistaken the pictured bombing for real. It's amazing how quickly a man reacts to fear. Three guys landed on top of me in a slit trench. Muggs asked me if next time I could bring a movie of Flo Ziegfeld's Follies.

In Espíritu, I met the commanding officer of a New Zealand fighter squadron located on an airstrip abandoned by the wing when the main strip was completed. We became friends, and soon I began swapping him American cigarettes for scotch and gin. Another bit of luck came along when I ran into a Seabee I had known on the Canal. While having a drink or two in my hut, he told me that, only that morning, the Seabees had unloaded two brand-new refrigerators and because there was no address on either, they had been stashed in a warehouse near the pier. (The Seabees had an icebox.) As soon as my friend left, I hastened to General Geiger's office and suggested to him a plan that could possibly allow us to latch on to the two boxes. The General thought enough of the plan to send his aide, Major Jack Cram, to fetch his second-in-command, General Louis Woods. By the time General Woods arrived, the plan was all set. General Woods and I, as his aide, along with four enlisted men were to drive to the warehouse in a truck. There, General Woods was to tell the guard that he had come to pick up two refrigerators that should have been addressed to the wing. General Geiger's hut was big enough for one of the boxes. The other just fit in the log affair, with my stove. We never discovered who was the rightful owner. Not that we tried!

On Espíritu Santo, near the Eleventh Marine Air Group airstrip, there was a small fresh water pool (off limits to enlisted men), over which extended the limb of a tree. From this limb hung a vine. I rigged a stick on the bottom of the vine and used it to swing out from the high side of the pool—and dive. One day there was a stranger in the pool when I arrived. After he saw me dive from the swing contraption, he said, "I think I'll have a go at that." He gave it a try and landed flat on his belly. It was the former flying-tiger pilot Pappy Boyington. He swam slowly ashore and hollered to me, "To hell with you and your damn gimmick."

In mid-March, I received a letter from Gene Markey, then stationed in Noumea on Admiral Halsey's staff. In his letter he bemoaned at length the fact that he had to leave me in the boondocks of Espíritu Santo but, as he put it, orders are orders—and he'd been told to go home. He was boarding a States-bound Navy cruiser in a day or so. He signed his letter "Poor lucky me."

A few days after I'd received the letter from Gene, I was knocking back a nightcap with General Geiger in his hut when he said, "Ben, I have to get an important dispatch back to Washington. What officer should I choose to deliver it?" "General," I answered, "there is but one officer to choose." The general broke in, "Who, you?" "Yes sir," said I, "that is exactly the officer I had in mind." Imagine my reaction when he continued, "Tell Tom Ennis to draw up your orders." (Colonel Tom Ennis was Wing operations officer.) Shortly after dawn, I was in the operations hut awaiting the arrival of the W-1.

When I repeated General Geiger's instructions to Colonel Ennis, I thought he'd faint. No officer had been ordered back to the States for any reason whatsoever since we'd set up camp on Espíritu. In an effort to hasten my way to Noumea, Colonel Ennis included in my orders a priority No. 1 for air travel. Actually he had meant priority No. 1 to Noumea, but the way the orders were written, the priority covered air travel anywhere. I forgot to mention that in those days air-travel priority No. 1 was issued only to the president and his cabinet!

I left Noumea in a government plane bound for San Francisco, with overnight stops on the islands of Fiji, Canton, Palmyra, and Honolulu. I was headed for San Diego to hitch a ride on a government plane to Washington. At the airport in San Francisco, I used my priority for the first time and got a great boot out of bouncing a nasty old man off the San Diego plane for having uttered something derogatory about the Marine Corps. My orders ensured me space in a plane leaving San Diego for Washington three days hence.

Having straightened out my transportation problem, I called Joan Bennett in Beverly Hills to tell her that I had run into her ex-husband in the Pacific and he'd soon be arriving in the States. Joan came back, "Gene's already home. He called me from San Francisco this morning and is coming for dinner tomorrow night. I'm asking as many of his old friends as I can locate. How about you? Can you make it?" I told her that I could—and would—be there, but not to mention it to Gene if she talked to him again.

I got to Joan's house a bit early to be sure to be on hand when Gene arrived. Stationing myself at the front door when it was opened for Gene, I greeted him with, "Well, well, if it isn't the poor lucky one! What took you so long?" With a look of utter bewilderment on his face he stammered, "W-where in hell did you come from?" It was those sort of things that helped make the war years bearable.

As General Geiger had told me that I needn't rush my return, after fulfilling my mission in Washington, I started back to Espíritu via New York. My longtime friend Bill Leeds was on leave from his duties in the Coast Guard and we painted the town red without even half trying. While lunching one day at 21 with Charlie Berns, chairman of 21 Brands, he asked me how the boys in the Pacific were doing for booze. When I answered, "Mainly doing without," he told me that maybe he could do something to rectify the situation. He volunteered to contact some of his West Coast liquor distributor friends to see if they couldn't deliver, in bond, some cases of booze to any spot I designated in San Francisco. "How many cases can they use?" he asked. Naturally I answered, "As many as you can come up with." What's more, he said he would guarantee payment until I could send him a check.

I wasn't at all sure that Charlie would be able to come up smiling, but taking no chances and hoping that he just might, I returned to Coronado via San Francisco. Once there, I had a long talk with the boys at 100 Harrison Street, the Fleet Marine Force, Pacific Headquarters. When I outlined the possibilities of obtaining the liquor, I was given the address of a safe warehouse to which any liquor addressed to the First Wing could be sent. They also assured me that they would see to it that the liquor was shipped, in bond, to Espíritu Santo. I called Charlie (God rest his soul) in New York, gave him the word, and thanked him again. While I was in San Francisco, an old friend of mine, Herbie Flieshackker, introduced me to a police captain who told me I could have six slot machines that had been confiscated as long as they were to be shipped out of the country. I had them delivered to the warehouse.

Back in Coronado to try and wangle a ride back to the Pacific, my Marine Corps luck still held when I learned that a plane from Espíritu Santo was bringing in General Geiger that very afternoon. He had been transferred to Washington. I met the plane at the gangway, reported to the general that his dispatch had been delivered, and recounted my other States-side efforts, including the possibility of the liquor shipment. When I mentioned that, he said, "I wish I was going back to Espíritu with you." The pilot of the general's plane was Colonel Elliot Bard from the Eleventh Marine Air Group, on Espíritu. When I asked the colonel if I could return with him, he answered, "Certainly. I'll be returning direct to Espíritu at 0900 one week from today." The delay bothered me not a whit as my wife was visiting Joan Bennett in Beverly Hills. By nightfall, Joan had two guests.

After a comfortable but uneventful trip back to the wing, I found that General Geiger had been relieved by General Patrick Mulcahy, a damned good officer—and, I was told, a handy man with a bottle. We immediately became friends when I told him of the liquor we might be getting from San Francisco. We became even better friends when I gave him three bottles of scotch I'd gotten from my New Zealand chum.

While I was away, the officer's club had somehow gotten hold of an ice-making machine, a fact that most certainly helped the iced-tea situation. However, on more than one occasion I had heard officers wonder out loud why the club couldn't come up with some pukka glasses. Iced tea served in thick issue glasses just didn't taste the same. One day, I noticed the *President Jackson* anchored in Bougainville Channel, and it gave me an idea.

In 1938, I had crossed the Pacific in the *President Jackson,* and I remembered that the purser didn't serve drinks in thick glasses. So down at the pier I climbed aboard a put-put and was chugg-chugged out to the *Jackson.* The same purser was aboard and apparently was glad to see me again. While drinking drinks served in thick issue glasses, I asked him what had happened to the thin glasses of yesteryear. "Oh," he answered, "they have been stored in the hold ever since the *Jackson* was converted into a troopship." In our conversation, the purser had mentioned how much he would like to glom onto a samurai sword. Knowing that my sergeant had one that he had picked up on the Canal, I asked, "If I can find a samurai sword, how about letting me trade it to you for the thin glasses in the hold." "Not all of them," he replied, "but maybe for a couple of gross. How'd that be?" Quickly I came back, "You've just made a deal, if I can find a sword."

Back on the Island, I explained the situation to my sergeant and asked him how much he wanted for his sword. "I hadn't thought about selling it," he responded, "but under the circumstances, I guess one hundred bucks would be a fair price." I then went to the officer's club and told them that I could get nearly two gross of thin glasses for $100. The club jumped at the opportunity, and the deal was made. Naturally, General Mulcahy got a dozen highball glasses (his favorite drink), and I held out a couple of dozen assorted glasses for myself. Now all the club had to do was find something besides tea to pour in the glasses.

The club's lack-of-liquor problem was temporarily solved a few days later when my New Zealand friend asked, "Do you think your officer's club could use ninety-five cases of scotch?" I answered him with a question: "Do all New

Zealanders ask such foolish questions?" He continued, "A close friend of mine is head man of immigration in Auckland, and this morning I received a letter from him stating that if I wanted ninety-five cases of Ne Plus Ultra scotch, I could have them at the in-bond price. I can't handle that much and wondered if you could." Apparently the scotch had been on its way from London to Hong Kong, but when the Japs took over Victoria Island, the ship carrying the liquor had been diverted to Auckland, and the liquor was still being held there, in bond. As the shipment had been slated for Hong Kong, it could not be disposed of in New Zealand. (The British are sticklers for that sort of thing.) My friend Anzie continued, "I'll give you a chit to my friend in Auckland, and I'm certain you'd have no problem in obtaining the scotch, as long as you are taking it out of the country." "Sit you down and start writing the chit while I pay General Mulcahy a visit," I told him.

In the general's office, I started off, "General, if I can pick up seventy or eighty cases of Ne Plus Ultra scotch for the officer's club, should I?" "What's holding you up?" the general came back. "Orders, transportation and dough," I answered. and went on to explain the possibility. "I'll have your orders written and arrange for the money," the general said. "You call the Eleventh and tell them that I said to wind up one of their transport planes." I didn't know how much dough I would need, but General Mulcahy figured that eighty cases of Ne Plus Ultra would cost somewhere around $30 per case and instructed the supply officer to give me $2,500 cash. I was off like a giant bird.

In Auckland, armed with the chit and the money, I headed straight for the immigration office, where I presented the chit to the head man, who couldn't have been more agreeable or cooperative. He asked me if I wanted the scotch loaded that afternoon, but thinking a night in Auckland was indicated, I told him that the next morning would be fine. When I told him that I'd like to pay for the scotch then and there he gave me the tab, and how much do you think it amounted to? Ninety-five cases of Ne Plus Ultra scotch, in bond, at $12.70 per case came to $1,206.50! At the airport the following morning, the scotch was loaded on the plane, along with ten assorted cases of booze like bourbon, gin, rum and vermouth, which I had purchased, also in bond, for $90.40. The plane lumbered down the airstrip and we were off for Espíritu. Five cases of scotch were dropped at my friend Anzie's quarters as a finder's fee, five cases at General Mulcahy's hut, and five assorted cases at my log hut. The officer's club ended up with ninety cases—and a $1203.10 refund. Drinks served in thin glasses tasted just like home.

Considering the wartime pressures bearing down on practically the entire world, by July 1943, Espíritu Santo had developed into a far-from-bad place to be. The climate was good, the foliage lush, and wild-pigeon shooting was excellent. One day, while doing something in front of my hut, I heard a voice behind me say, "Swahili." Knowing but one person who called me that, I knew it had to be Jack Bergen—and, sure enough, it was. He had come to Espíritu for a confab with Admiral Halsey, whose headquarters had been set up next to the Wing's. Jack had brought two bottles of Ballantine scotch, one of which we started working on in my hut. "I'm glad you are here," I told him, "because to-night I'm having a barbecue party. I'll pick you up and take you."

Helped greatly by my French patois, I had become friendly with a congenial French lady, Madame Gardel, whose house and grounds were on the north shore of Palikoola Bay. Once or twice, she had her chef roast some pigeons for me and, when she asked if I'd like two wild boars, she gave me the idea for a barbecue. Besides Jack Bergen, my guests included Generals Mulcahy, Woods, and Ralph Mitchell, Admiral Halsey and his aide, plus twenty other hungry friends of mine. The barbecued boars and a couple of dozen roasted pigeon ensured a sufficiency of food, and the bar, plenty of hooch. Near the beach, a long table was rigged under an overhanging limb of a banyan tree, from which hung Japanese lanterns. Chairs, chinaware, the tablecloth, napkins and glasses, I had borrowed from the officer's club, the knives and forks, from Madame Gardel. I must say the entire ensemble made quite an attractive setting. Six musicians from the wing band kept things lively. I wasn't quite sure which impressed Jack Bergen the most—the four-foot-wide half of a giant clam shell filled with ice and topped with oysters on the half shell, the Waring mixer on the bar, or the whole layout—but at one point during the evening, he said to me, "If I'd known that the war in the Pacific was anything like this, I'd have been out here long ago."

Two days after the barbecue bash, a gunnery sergeant came to my hut and presented a bill of lading for 260 cases of liquor that had been shipped to me in bond from San Francisco, along with six slot machines, in the passenger-cargo ship *Trenton,* anchored in Bougainville Channel. The gunny also gave me a letter addressed to 100 Harrison Street containing an invoice from Charlie Berns and informing me that he had been able to obtain 150 cases of scotch, 70 cases of bourbon, and 40 cases of assorted liquor, and he hoped it would be enough to help. Oh boy! Was it!

When I asked the gunny what time the *Trenton* had dropped her hook, and he answered, "Aboot daybreak," I knew I was talking to a Virginian and asked him what part of Virginia he was from. When he said, "Petersburg," an immediate rapport was established. He went on to tell me that he and a platoon of gyrenes had been shipped out as replacements to the wing and put aboard the *Trenton* with implicit orders to maintain a running guard on the liquor shipment. He said, "If you'll arrange for transportation to meet us on the pier, I'll have the platoon unload the lot and deliver it to any spot on the island you designate." Within ten minutes, three trucks were on their way to the pier.

I then hastened to General Pat's office to inform him of our godsend and ask where the liquor could be stored. He thought for a moment and then said, "We'll store it in the brig until a safe place can be arranged at the officer's club." I dispatched my sergeant to the pier to guide the gunny directly to the brig. After the liquor was stacked within the barbed-wire brig enclosure, the gunny dropped by my hut with additional good news. "Don't be surprised, captain," he said, "if you find that you have eighty cases of bourbon instead of seventy. I had the boys filch ten cases from an unguarded liquor shipment nearby in the hold, addressed to some Army outfit in New Caledonia." Naturally I made certain that the gunny got the job he wanted in the Wing. General Pat wanted to commission him!

The general arranged with the paymaster to draw a check charged to the club to Charles Berns, covering the amount of the invoice. The check I enclosed in a letter full of thanks to Charlie, along with a picture I had taken of a squad of men with bayoneted rifles standing guard on the liquor. On the back of the picture, I had written, "To give you an idea of how closely we guard your thoughtfulness."

Even before the liquor was moved from the brig into a sort of basement vault dug under the club, the slot machines were starting to pay for it. Somehow, somebody got hold of a large supply of quarters, and the two-bit slot machines were eating them up from noon to midnight. As the only place on Espíritu with a supply of booze *and* slot machines, the Wing officer's club quickly became the most popular spot on the island. The enlisted men did all right too, using American cigarettes to trade to the natives for wine. I don't know how much profit the slot machines eventually showed, but I do know that, by the time I left the Pacific some four months after they were installed, they had made enough to pay for a large part of the liquor bill. They had also helped enable the club to charge only twenty cents for drinks! I learned later that before the vault under the club was completely empty, a certain amount of booze had become available from ships in the channel.

In Beverly Hills, on my return from the trek to Washington, I was introduced to Judy Garland. I asked her point-blank if she would consider coming to the Pacific in the New Hebrides and Solomon Islands area to sing for the troops, if I could make arrangements with the USO. She answered that she'd love to as soon as she finished an up-coming picture.

Toward the end of August, on my way to the Russell Islands, I stopped off on Guadalcanal for a couple of days and spent my first evening dining with Gilbert Kahn at his naval officer's mess. During dinner, I told the group not to be surprised if one day soon Judy Garland stepped down from a plane on Henderson Field. I had not heard from her, but was still hoping. Sometime during the evening, I was told that the Third Marine Division had landed on the Canal at Koli Point to stage for the upcoming invasion of Bougain-ville, and knowing that Bob Kriendler was in the Head-quarter's Battalion of the Third Division, the next day I borrowed a jeep and took off for Koli Point, some ten to twelve miles east of Henderson Field. As a gift, I took with me something that I was fairly certain Bob hadn't seen in a long time, the other bottle of Ballantine scotch that Jack Bergen had given me. At Koli Point, I found not only Bob

Pouring a drink of Ballantine's for Bob Kriendler in front of Jack and Charlie's "21," S.W. Pacific, Koli Point, 1943

but Malcolm Byer and George Percy, who were also in the Third Division. We toasted the boys on Fifty-second Street with drinks poured out of what was probably the first bottle of Ballantine ever on Guadalcanal. It's always nice to run into friends anywhere, but in such an unlikely place, it is particularly gratifying. As I was arriving back at Henderson Field, a lieutenant commander, one of the group of the previous evening, flagged me down. After I'd braked to a stop, he said, "Judy Garland has certainly changed in looks, hasn't she?" To my, "What do you mean?" he answered, "The first white woman to set foot on Guadalcanal since the Japs took over walked down the gangway of a plane on Henderson Field around noon." It hadn't been Judy Garland; it was Eleanor Roosevelt!

I had done time on Guadalcanal when the going was rough and had been in the South Pacific for more than a year when I received a communication from the New York Draft Board instructing me to report to Grand Central Terminal for a physical examination, preparatory to being inducted into the Armed Forces. My reply was axiomatic. I wrote across the bottom of their letter, "Too late," and signed it, "Ben Finney, Captain, USMCR, South Pacific." That was as near as I ever came to being drafted in any war.

Some months before I had received another mixed-up communication from the war-risk insurance people, in which they informed me that I had been born in 1899; my World War I enlistment papers so stated. Pushing my age back a year in order to enlist in the first "war to end all wars" had come back to haunt me. Fortunately, I had a copy of my birth certificate verifying the fact that the year of my birth was 1900. I enclosed the certificate with their letter, which I returned, and that was that. Apparently, the Marine Corps had ignored the age discrepancy when I applied for a commission.

My tour of duty in the Southwest Pacific ended at Munda, on New Georgia Island, in early December, 1943. When General Mulcahy had been transferred to Munda he took me with him. Actually, I wasn't there long enough to find out what I was supposed to do, but I did find time for a look-see at the nearby islands of Rendova and Vella Lavella.

I flew back to the States via Fiji, Samoa, Canton, Palmyra, and Honolulu. In San Francisco, I finagled a ride in an Army transport plane to Fort Dix. On the way from Dix to Trenton, where I was going to catch a train to New York, the car I was in tangled with a light tank, and I received my only "wound" in World War II: a badly strained shoulder. Fortunately my "wound" wasn't serious enough to call for a disability discharge. After a month's leave, I was ordered to report to Coronado, where I was assigned the job of morale officer for all the air stations on the West Coast.

While visiting air stations like El Toro, El Centro, Mohave, and Santa Barbara, I ran across quite a few men who had been well-known football players on both pro and college teams. Figuring that football came under morale, I started wondering just how the football players could be gotten together in one spot. The answer came in the spring of 1944, when Colonel Dick Hanley arrived at Camp Pendleton to set up a West Coast combat-conditioning training unit. I drove up to Pendleton to have a talk with one of the best football coaches Northwestern University ever had, Dick Hanley. I told him about the number of ex-football players scattered around the air stations and my thoughts concerning the possibility of a Marine football team. I also suggested that, if possible, it might be a good idea if he could persuade Washington to let him set up his unit at El Toro instead of Pendleton, mainly because the nearby stadium in Santa Anna could be used as a home field, and there was a plethora of air transportation available at El Toro. He cottoned to the suggestion and somehow arranged to switch from Pendleton to El Toro. I arranged to switch from the job of morale officer to executive officer of combat conditioning on the West Coast and also moved to El Toro.

Pretty soon, football-playing Marines from all over were being transferred to El Toro to go through the combat-conditioning course and become combat-conditioning instructors. When they had completed their training course, it was my job to spot them around the various air stations. The ones Dick Hanley put his finger on weren't spotted. They stayed at El Toro—players like Cliff Battles and "Wee Willie" Wilkin of the Washington Redskins, Bob Dove from Notre Dame, Paul Governali from Columbia, and Hugh Galleaneau from Stanford, to mention a few. I even tried to get "Moose" Krouse, of Notre Dame fame, to transfer from San Diego, but he didn't want to leave San Diego. With Dick Hanley as their coach, the El Toro Marines became a football team to be reckoned with. (No college team would dare book us.) But service teams from March Field, Denver, El Paso, Alameda, and Randolph Field in Texas were played—and defeated.

In the spring of the last year of the war, I was still stationed at El Toro. Muriel had an apartment in Beverly Hills, and, with gasoline rationing keeping the civilian traffic down, it was a breeze to drive the forty-odd miles in less than an hour. I spent nearly every weekend in Beverly with her and often drove up for dinner at Chasen's or Romanoff's on weekday nights. I was living high on the hog and had become quite convinced that this was the way a war should be fought when, out of the wild blue yonder, a dispatch arrived ordering me to report to Ewa, a Marine air station near Honolulu, for further overseas duty.

As I had already spent sixteen months in the South Pacific and had thought I'd be safe at El Toro for the rest of the war, the dispatch came as a distinct shock. Through my spies, I soon discovered that General Patrick Mulcahy, then in Ewa, had been looking for an aide to accompany him on the upcoming invasion of Okinawa. Apparently, my name had been suggested to him by a member of his staff, Colonel "Fish" Salmon, who I had thought till then was a friend of mine.

Recognizing orders as orders, I packed my gear and headed for Fleet Marine Force, Pacific Headquarters, in

San Francisco, to obtain transportation to Honolulu. After scouting around Headquarters, I learned that General Mulcahy was slated to leave Ewa for Guam at 0700 two days hence, which meant that, if I could delay my departure to Honolulu for twenty-four hours, I would not arrive in Ewa until after he had shoved off. So, when I presented my orders to the transportation officer, I asked if I could possibly be off-loaded until the following night, as I had urgent business in San Francisco. I failed to mention anything about General Mulcahy. The transportation officer was a good joe for whom I'd done a favor in Espiritu Santo. He was happy to return the favor.

The big, old flying boat put down in Pearl Harbor at 0630, half an hour before General Pat was due to leave Ewa for Guam. I'll admit that I dawdled a bit over a cup of coffee, nor did I tell the driver to hurry while being driven the twelve miles to Ewa. Anyway, it was 0730 when I reported to General Moore, the commanding general at Ewa. The general had a proclivity to cock his head to one side when he spoke. It was pretty well cocked when he asked, "What in hell took you so long? General Mulcahy was looking for you." Laying my orders on his desk, I pointed to the fact that I had been off-loaded in San Francisco. "Fish" Salmon had left with General Mulcahy, and all I could find out was that he had thought it very funny. Ha! Ha! I forget just how, but eventually I got even with Colonel Salmon.

I was hoping that I'd be returned to El Toro, but two days later General Moore sent for me and read aloud a very concise dispatch: "Order Major Finney to report to me in Guam—Mulcahy." I could feel the rug being pulled from under me as he continued: "I'm having your orders written. There is a plane leaving fro Guam at noon. You have three days to catch him, and *by God*, this time you won't be off-loaded!"

It was a two-and-a-half-day haul from Ewa to Guam, with overnight stops at Johnston and Engebi islands. I had begun to think that my San Francisco maneuver had been in vain

101

when I found out that our pilot took a rather dim view of General Mulcahy. His reason was that somewhere along the line the general had punished him for what he, the pilot, thought was a very minor infraction. It gave me an idea!

Sitting in the copilot's seat en route from Johnston to Engebi, I casually let drop, "Doesn't that starboard inboard motor sound out of sync to you?" "What do you mean?" he quickly asked. And I told him my problem. My hopes soared when he said, "Maybe you're right about that motor." I knew I was home free when I heard him tell the crew chief that we'd lay over in Engebi the following day to have the inboard starboard motor checked. I was further elated the next day when I heard from an Ewa-bound pilot from Guam that General Mulcahy's convoy was shoving off for Okinawa that evening.

Upon my arrival in Guam, I did my best to locate General Mulcahy, but was informed that he had left for Okinawa the night before. So I returned to Ewa in the same plane with the same pilot who, incidentally, was later made a major general. It couldn't have happened to a more deserving guy.

When I reported back to General Moore, his head was really cocked over to one side as he said, "Well, you've done it again! I don't know how th' hell you do it, but it's a good thing for the Corps that not many Marines know how to operate like you do." Obviously, he had overlooked the fact that what a man learns in one war about how to operate is seldom forgotten in another.

For some reason, General Moore was determined that I not get back to El Toro, and for two weeks I did little more than wait for something to happen. It happened when two ground colonels from Washington turned up at Ewa and requested a plane to fly them on an inspection trip to the South Pacific. I was detailed to accompany them as an "air host," whatever that was.

Our route to Guam was practically identical with my abortive effort of two weeks before. From Guam, we kept on to the islands of Tinian, Saipan, Ulithi, and Peleliu. At

Peleliu, it was very obvious that the Marines had had real tough going. Returning through Guam, I ran into Bob Kriendler, who was on General Graves Erskine's staff. This time, he provided the bottle of Ballantine out of which we drank to various mutual friends.

Leaving Guam, we headed south to Bougainville, Guadalcanal, and Espíritu Santo. The last two brought back recent memories. The Canal was crisscrossed with crushed gravel roads, but I noticed that the black dust was still around. The former Wing headquarters on Espíritu reminded me of a country club.

One of the colonels on the tour of inspection was a football buff and knew all about the El Toro Marines. I told him how very much I wanted to get back to El Toro to prepare for the upcoming football season and asked him if he could please arrange for my transfer back in Washington. He told me that he'd try.

While awaiting my hoped-for orders back at Ewa, I must have had something to do with morale as I remember flying a group of entertainers headed by Captain Ray Heatherton to Midway Island in an effort to break the monotony of the Marines stationed on such a lonely spot. In a way, I'm glad my orders didn't come through until they did, because it enabled me to witness one of the most moving experiences of all time, certainly to Americans, the crippled U.S.S. *Franklin*'s arrival alongside a Pearl Harbor dock. Weeks before, off Okinawa, two Japanese kamikaze pilots had gone down trying to take the carrier with them. One did manage to set her ablaze from stem to stern, wounding her badly. Stories of how her heroic volunteer crew had subdued the fires and were nursing her listing hull across the Pacific to Pearl Harbor had preceded her. Every gob and gyrene who could, along with the base's combined Navy and Marine bands, crowded on a dock to welcome her.

Morris and Sidney Legendre, old friends of mine, were stationed at Pearl Harbor with Naval Intelligence and took me with them to the top of the docking tower to watch the

U.S.S. Franklin, *after being hit by a kamikaze off Okinawa, 1945*

Franklin's arrival. As the badly listing, battle-scarred carrier made fast just below us, the combined bands broke into "Anchors Aweigh," accompanied by roars of welcome from all hands. When the music and cheers subsided, from the canted deck of the *Franklin* a makeshift band composed of a trumpet, a saxophone, six or eight guys with combs and tissue paper, another two or three using tin pans as drumheads, answered with "God Bless America." There wasn't a dry eye in the house!

Several years later, I wrote a story for a motion picture based on the above, with the idea of Frank Sinatra being cast in the lead role as *Trumpet Smith*, the title I'd put on the tale. Frank read the script and was more than willing to play the part, but unfortunately this was before his memorable comeback in *From Here to Eternity*—and not a studio in Hollywood would touch him. Eventually I sold the story to Paramount, who in turn sold it to Columbia, who finally made it with the title changed to *Battle Stations*.

My orders finally came through, ordering me back to El Toro, and I took off with the speed of an antelope. Dick Hanley welcomed me as though he meant it. The combat-conditioning training courses were still functioning, and practically all of the 1944 football players were still aboard. Pretty soon, Elroy "Crazylegs" Hirsh, Mickey McArdle, and Laverne Gagne reported to El Toro, making the forthcoming football season look even better. On December 9, 1945, in the Los Angeles Coliseum, the undefeated El Toro Marines played the undefeated Fleet City Blue-jackets for the mythical service championship, before a crowd of 84,000 fans.

I doubt that there has ever been a football game in which at one time during the game twelve All-Americans were facing each other on one team or the other. The Navy's Buddy Young, "Mr. Five-by-Five," never had a better day, and I'm certain it was the only case on record when one flatfoot whupped eleven gyrenes. Receiving the opening kickoff, he raced the entire length of the field for a touchdown. In the second quarter, he took a punt on his twenty-yard line and ran for another score. In spite of Mr. Young, at half-time, the score was tied 21 to 21.

Both teams scored early in the third quarter, and the stands were going crazy. Bob Hope, who was sitting directly behind Bill Powell, hit William so many times on the head with his program that Bill tried to change seats with his wife. The cad! In the fourth quarter, Buddy Young, taking a punt on his twenty-five-yard line, reversed his field twice and slithered along a sideline to score yet again. In the unbelieving hush that followed, a Marine in the stands voiced most of our thoughts when he shouted at the top of his lungs, "It's a goddam lie!"

As much as I hate to admit it, the final score was Fleet City, 41, El Toro, 35. But it was without question one of the most exciting football classics ever played anywhere. Ask Bob Hope.

After nearly four years of active service, I was discharged at El Toro in February, 1946, and made a beeline for my adopted home—New York City.

If I have given the impression that I spent as much time procuring liquor as I did fighting in World War II, so be it. I worked on the theory that being able to get a shot was equally as important as getting shot at.

Marine Corps participation in World War II was mostly in the Pacific theatre of operation where it did a bang-up job, as I'm certain most countries will agree, especially Japan.

As I should hate for anyone to gather the impression that my activities in that war typified those of all Marines, I would like to point out here that I learned a lot in World War I about what could or could not be done in wartime, which helped me a lot in the Pacific showdown. What's more, I had a Purple Heart and didn't want another. However, I did do time on Guadalcanal when the going was the toughest and very easily could have procured a star for my purple ribbon.

Fortunately, comparatively few Marines who served their country in the Second World War had seen action in the first. Otherwise victory in the Pacific might have taken longer.

Incidentally, each and every officer I have mentioned in this chapter accomplished many things for the good of the Corps. I will not list their accomplishments. I'll just say, they were all *good* Marines!

Three weeks of active duty, El Toro, summer of 1947

8 | Again – Between Wars

DURING THE FALL OF THE YEAR I WAS DISCHARGED, I READ
Ravenel's *Tap Roots*, a story about how a family in Mississippi defended their valley home against the Yankees in the
war between the states, and thought it might make a good
motion picture. I wrote Walter Wanger just that in a note
enclosed with a copy of *Tap Roots*. Walter, at the time, was
producing pictures at Universal Studios in Burbank,
California. He read the book, agreed with me that it would

make a good picture, and called asking me to contact the author's agent with regard to purchasing the movie rights. I contacted the agent, talked to him, and so informed Walter. He took it from there. A month or so later, Walter called to tell me that the rights had been purchased and asked if I would come out to Universal as executive producer on the film. So a year after I'd left California, I was back again!

My first job was to fly in Walter's private plane to Mississippi to try to locate the valley described in *Tap Roots*. After flying back and forth over the state for hours, I was unable to locate anything that even vaguely resembled such a valley. That evening, while dining with Mike O'Leary, manager of the Saint Charles Hotel in New Orleans, I was introduced to a chap from Asheville, North Carolina. When I told him about my disappointing day, he said, "I read *Tap Roots*, and there's a valley near Asheville that could be, I think, just what you are looking for." He was returning to Asheville the next day, and not only accompanied me but drove me out for a ground look at the valley. As we looked around, my friend said, "You see what I mean?" And I certainly did. It was perfect. We found the owner who very nicely gave me an agreement for Walter, stating that he could use the valley for location shots. Walter was very pleased with the results of my effort, and particularly pleased with pictures I had taken of the valley and the agreement I had gotten from its owner.

I helped work on the movie script and spent the rest of my time trying to act like an Executive Producer. Even before the script was finished, casting had begun, and I must say Walter came up with a good one: Susan Hayward and Van Heflin in the lead roles, supported by Boris Karloff, Ward Bond, Julie London, and Richard Long. Chosen as director was the great George Marshall, with Dick Templeton as his assistant.

The script called for one take of a confederate battery of cannon firing a salvo. As we were preparing to leave for Asheville, I happened to hear that prop cannons would be taken with us, whereupon I opened my big mouth and told

George Marshall that prop cannons would not be necessary, as the real things could be found on nearly every courthouse lawn throughout the south. The prop cannons were left behind.

Everything was copacetic until the day neared when the confederate battery would be needed. I had sent scouts to every courthouse lawn in the vicinity of Asheville looking for cannon; they came up empty! Finally, I was told that most confederate cannons had been melted down for metal during World War II. After learning of this sad state of affairs, I happened to run into an old friend of mine who had been a cadet at Virginia Military Institute when I was a student at the university. When I told him about the inaccessibility of confederate cannon and why, he said, "I know where there's one confederate battery that sure as hell wasn't melted down: Stonewall Jackson's original battery at the foot of his statue on one end of the parade ground at VMI." I could have kissed him. The following morning at the break of dawn I was off for Lexington, Virginia.

VMI was closed for the summer, but I located the acting superintendent and asked him if I could borrow Jackson's battery for ten days. I told him how badly it was needed in a motion picture being filmed to the west, near the Virginia–North Carolina border. I didn't say which side of the state line. Actually it was just a little white lie of sorts, as Asheville isn't very far below the border. "Mr. Finney," he said, "there is no way that I could let Stonewall Jackson's battery leave the institute's campus without permission from the governor, or Secretary of State General George Marshall, who also happens to be president of the institute's board of governors. Jackson's original battery rates damned near as high as Patrick Henry or Robert E. Lee in the lore of the State of Virginia. The battery is practically sacred."

Immediately I put a call through to the governor, only to be told that he was on his vacation. The superintendent very nicely volunteered to get General Marshall on the phone. Fortunately, I remembered that the general had roomed with my uncle, Charlie Kennon, while a cadet at VMI. I started the conversation by saying, "General, this is Charlie Kennon's nephew speaking," and went on to tell him how badly the battery was needed. The general broke in: "Charlie Kennon's nephew can have anything he wants. Let me speak to the superintendent." I intimated above that the Super was a nice chap, and he further proved it when he said that he'd call a moving-van outfit in Staunton and tell them to send a large van to transport the battery.

When the van arrived, the battery was loaded aboard, and I told the driver to follow me. The cannon were unloaded at the spot where they would be lined up for the salvo, and I told the driver that I'd call him when it was time to pick the battery up and return it to VMI. By no means did I want it returned in a van bearing a North Carolina license plate. I also asked him not to mention Asheville, and if he wouldn't, I'd have autographed pictures of Susan Hayward and Van Heflin to give him upon his return.

I had just made the deadline, because the next day the battery was ready to defend the south. Extras in confederate uniforms were all in place and so were the cameras. I was watching as the command was given: "Ready. Aim. Fire." BOOM! the cannon let go—and so did three of the wooden gun carriages and wheels! They completely collapsed! Right then, I knew that I'd never again be able to visit my home state of Virginia.

That night, I was practically crying when I told my Asheville friend what had happened. "Wait a minute," he said, "didn't you tell me that only three of the gun carriages had collapsed? Well, there's an old wagon maker on the edge of town who is still plying his trade. Why couldn't he use the intact cannon as a model and fashion three new carriages?" The following morning I had the intact cannon and the three cannon barrels trucked to the wagon maker and followed in my car. When I explained to him what I hoped he could do, he asked, "Why not let me make four new gun carriages and wheels. I'll paint them all the same color and then they'd look alike."

On the last day of my ten-day loan, the battery was back in

Lexington. That same evening, I called the superintendent at VMI to make sure it had arrived safely and to tell him, with fear and trepidation, what had happened. You can imagine my relief when he responded, "That's wonderful, Mr. Finney. We had been wondering for some time how long the many coats of paint would hold the old wood together. You have solved our problem, and—thanks." Stonewall Jackson may think that he is standing over his "original" battery, but he ain't. And I have visited the State of Virginia many times since.

One of the crew searched through the debris and picked up two of the largest pieces of the undercarriages he could find, took them back to California, fashioned them into bookends, and presented them to me. It was a very nice gesture, but as they reminded me of something I was trying to forget, the two pieces of Stonewall Jackson's original battery are now on exhibit in the Marine commandant's house in Washington, a gift from the guy who made it possible.

Back at Universal, with retakes dubbed in and the film edited, *Tap Roots* became an accomplished fact. I then decided to branch out on my own and produce films for television, an up-and-coming departure from standard filmmaking. Tying up with Bill Menzies, an eminent Hollywood writer and director, I formed a company and started filming at the Hal Roach Studios in Culver City. In those early days of producing films strictly for television, no one seemed to be certain of the preferred length, fifteen minutes or thirty minutes. For our first attempt we had chosen a short story written by Edgar Allan Poe, "The Telltale Heart." It fit in a fifteen-minute time slot and, as it would have been difficult to pad Poe, we let it go at that. At the first ceremony of the Academy of Television Arts and Sciences, we were awarded a Certificate of Merit for our effort. We made three more fifteen-minute films, including Wilkie Collins's "Terribly Strange Bed," with Richard Long in the lead spot. Unfortunately, we found out too late that thirty-minute films were being demanded.

For some time, I'd had a burning desire to plant my feet once again on the sidewalks of New York, so when my desire got so hot I couldn't stand it any longer, I packed my gear and headed east.

Stonewall Jackson's original battery at VMI

9 | And Then Came Korea

IT WAS NOW 1952, AND THE KOREAN FRACAS HAD SHIFTED
into high gear. I was happily settled in New York, minding
my own business. Then, in July, I received a dispatch that
shocked me, this time from Washington. It read: "At 0800,
August 4, 1952, you will report to U. S. Marine Headquarters, Washington, D.C., for active duty." As a reserve
officer, I had had two or three weeks of active duty each
summer since 1946, never dreaming that I'd ever be called

back to active duty for real. My first reaction was that the country must really be in one hell of a fix if they were calling back fifty-two-year-old reserve officers for active duty.

My next action was to put through a call to Lem Shepherd, an old Virginia friend of mine, and then commandant of the Marine Corps, to find out if there'd been some kind of mistake. "Lem," I started, "I received a dispatch this morning from Washington." "You did?" he said. "Read it to me." I did. "Let's see, August fourth is next Friday. I'll see you Friday. You'll like Korea." Normally, that would be the end of conversation between a reserve officer and his commandant, but since Lem was a longtime friend, I kept on talking. "Korea, did you say? At my age, what in hell could I do to help in Korea?" "We were looking for a reserve officer who has served with both land and air groups to write a report on how land and air are functioning on the Main Line of Resistance, and when your name popped up, you were chosen. I'll see you Friday."

At 0800, on August 4, 1952, I reported to Marine Headquarters and, exactly twelve hours later, was on my way to Korea. The commandant had very thoughtfully arranged for me to hitch a ride with General Al Pollack, who was on his way to relieve, as it happened, a relative of mine, General John Selden, commanding general of the First Division in Korea.

After seven days of uneventful air travel, with overnight stops along the way, the plane put down in Seoul, where I changed into a chopper and was whirled off to the Main Line of Resistance (MLR). As a sort of added starter, I was more or less on my own and, because I was, chose to report to the commanding officer of the Fifth Regiment, my old outfit from World War I days. Colonel Eustace Smoak was commanding the regiment and made me welcome. His headquarters camp was just below the top of the ridge that marked the MLR and was comparatively sheltered from enemy fire. However, shells did pass overhead now and then and, on two occasions, landed in the camp, but luckily

Commandant Lem Shepherd, 1952.

Commandant Shepherd swearing me in as a light colonel, 1952

General Oscar Brice and Commandant Shepherd pinning on my silver leaves, 1952

they caused no casualties. Several times I visited my old battalion, the First, then commanded by Major Al Gentleman and found that my old company, which Lem Shepherd had commanded in France, was commanded by his son in Korea.

Just how I figured that flying over the enemy lines would help in my report I can't remember, but one fine day I climbed into the rear seat of one of the daily reconnaissance planes and we took off. As we were flying directly over the North Korean lines at about two thousand feet, antiaircraft shells started bursting all around us. When one shell burst near enough to shake the plane, I tapped the pilot on his back and hollered, "Do these things ever hit you?" He helped a lot when he hollered back, "Not yet."

Another day, General Pollack stopped by the camp, and as he was leaving, asked me if I would like to accompany him on a jeep ride along the base of the ridge. We headed west and stopped several times, once to watch helicopters as they brought back the wounded from outpost Baker which was located between the lines on the enemy side of the ridge. Continuing on toward the west, we noticed that the ridge turned a bit to the south and sloped down, but no one had told us that the sloping ridge allowed enemy cannon to zero in on one particular area. We must have entered that particular area, as all of a sudden our jeep was bracketed by two enemy shells, one in front, one behind. I hit the ground running, and ran so fast I could hardly hear a voice behind me holler, "Run!" Crouched down on the east side of a big rock I could plainly tell that, inadvertently, I had heeded my cousin's third bit of advice about being ready for anything.

Many of you will remember that, following the Inchon landing that was conceived by General McArthur, executed by the First Marine Division, and supported by the First Marine Air Wing, the Marines continued their advance to the Yalu River but were forced to withdraw under overwhelming pressure by Chinese Communist forces. The Communists kept pushing to the Chosen Reservoir, where General Lem Shepherd so distinguished himself. After the battle of the reservoir, a new MLR was established running east from Panmunjom and was never breached.

With the final period on my report, I left the MLR and headed south for Pohang, the headquarters site of the First Marine Aircraft Wing commanded by General Jerry Jerome, to wangle transportation home. I presented my orders and, in turn, was presented a cable addressed to General Jerome and signed by General Shepherd. The last sentence read, "Tell Ben Finney he can return to the States with me." Apparently, the commandant was arriving in two weeks on an inspection tour. While awaiting the commandant's arrival, I was sent to arrange details at each South Korean military installation he was slated to visit during his inspection tour.

As an example of what a small world it is, while driving around the airfield in Pusan I noticed a sign in front of a

Sign at end of runway, Pohang, Korea, 1952

building: "Headquarters—South African Air Force." By the sign were standing two lieutenants and, on the off-chance, I asked, "Would either of you happen to know a Major Durston in Capetown?" Just then, an officer walked out of the building. Pointing to him, one of the lieutenants said, "There's the colonel now!" It was Durston, the chap I'd met twelve years before aboard a South African troopship en route to Kenya!

Carrying on with coincidences, after the commandant arrived, I accompanied him on his tour of inspection. While inspecting the hangar of a night-fighter squadron, located just below the MLR, I couldn't help but notice that a not-too-young master tech sergeant kept looking at me. As we

General Jerry Jerome,
Pohang, Korea, 1952

were leaving the hangar, this sergeant approached me and said, "Pardon me, Colonel Finney, but were you in Base Hospital Six in Limoges just after the First World War?" "I was," I answered, whereupon he said, "By God! I knew it. I was in the next bed!" If *General* Finney hadn't visited me in the ward, I doubt that he would have remembered the name. I repeat—it's a small world.

All in all, the Korean fiasco struck me as being nothing more than a needless waste of thousands of American lives (over fifty-two thousand) and billions of American dollars, defending a country that few Americans had heard of until the start of the so-called war. Even now, we are still pouring billions of dollars into Korea for—what? Every time I think about it, I get a pain in my you know what, and I wasn't wounded in that war.

When the commandant's plane took off from the airfield in Seoul, the passengers aboard, besides the commandant, included General Oscar Brice; two other staff officers; "Bo," the commandant's son; and myself. After two days in Tokyo we left for Taipei, Formosa, where we lunched with Chiang Kai-Shek and, after lunch, carried on to Taiwan in southern Formosa for a day's visit with the Chinese Nationalist Marines. We arrived in Hong Kong in time to attend the horse races at the Repulse Bay racecourse. That evening we dined with the governor-general.

The next day we flew to Manila for a two-day layover at the Naval Headquarters on the island of Cavite in Manila Bay. On our first day at Cavite we sunned, swam, and lunched off the island of Corregidor. Our second day was spent on a flight up to Subic Bay for a look at the ill-fated American hospital ship which, during World War II, Jap bombs had reduced to nothing more than a burned-out hull. After Cavite, with daylong stops at Guam and Kwajalein, we arrived at Honolulu for a two-day stop. On the last leg of our trip to Washington, we stopped over in San Francisco for a night.

If I learned little else from the Korean fracas, I definitely learned that flying to war with one general and flying back with another is the only way to get in and out of a war. I shall forever be grateful to Lem Shepherd.

My last years as a reservist were joyous ones, up to a point. They included shooting birds all around the country and an African safari with Frank Hunter and the Duncan McMartins.

It was on this safari that I gave up shooting big game—or any animal, for that matter. We were camped on the Tana

The author and Frank Hunter, Tanganyika, British East Africa, 1958

Frank Hunter, Hilda McMartin, and myself on African safari, 1958

River, in northwestern Kenya. Frank had gone down one bank of the Tana looking for something to shoot, and Hilda and Dunc down the other, when native trackers arrived in camp to report that they had spotted five *big* elephants about five miles to the north. (They were always *big.*) I didn't particularly want to shoot an elephant, as I had already taken two large tuskers on previous safaris. However, since it was our last day on safari, I forced myself to take a look.

One of the five elephants did have fairly large ivory, so I let him have a .505 slug in his heart. As I watched the majestic beast, which had done nothing to me, quiver and shake before he went down, I knew right then that I had shot my last animal. And I haven't shot one since. Nowadays, every time I look at a picture of a beautiful lion or a beautiful tiger, I get tears in my eyes when I think that I contributed even to a small extent to the near-extinction of these beautiful cats. A small solace to big game hunters of the past is the fact that today's scarcity of game has been brought about much more by natives than by sportsmen.

I returned to the Isle of Pines in Cuba where, unbe-

El Colony Hotel, Isle of Pines, Cuba, 1958

knownst, catastrophe was awaiting me. I had spent two and a half years constructing a resort development on the Isle of Pines, which opened on December 28th, 1958. Three days after I opened the El Colony, Castro took over Cuba and I was out of business.

All transportation and even communications came to a distinct halt, and, during a daylong general strike ordered by Castro, hotel guests had to serve themselves and wash dishes. However, with the aid of Mario and Walter, two captains from 21 that Bob Kriendler had loaned me to help with the opening, and the French chef (they didn't have to join the strike), we made do. On January 5, my New York guests were able to get back in a chartered plane. I chose to remain on the island to see what could be salvaged. It was a wasted effort. Three weeks later, when I was informed that Castro had his eye on me, I left in the middle of the night via fishing boat and ended up in Palm Beach. I haven't been south of Miami since. And I also ended up with the dubious distinction of being known as the only person in the world who ever put on a revolution as a floor show.

Despite my other carryings-on, I managed to find time

most every year to do my active duty stints. My last stint was at Guantanamo, where I tried to figure why in hell the Marines stationed there hadn't been turned loose and headed west to handle Castro. At that stage of the game, many Cubans were anti-Castro, and had they been given the opportunity to join up with the Marines, there is no question that I wouldn't have had to leave the Isle of Pines.

Returning from "Gitmo," I stopped in Washington and had lunch at Marine Headquarters with General Randolph Pate, then commandant. Randy Pate and I had been friends since the days he was a cadet at VMI and I was a student at the university. During lunch he asked, "You are due to retire soon, aren't you?" I answered, "Yes, why?" "I'll tell you why," he kept on, "there is only one other reserve officer left in the Corps who served with the Fifth Regiment in France. He is practically dying, so why don't you wait to retire until he is in Arlington Cemetery, then you'd be the last." Randy arranged to hold up my retirement, and the following November, I *was* the last. I retired on December 1, 1960.

10 A Bit of This and a Bit of That

WHILE I MAY HAVE DWELT AT LENGTH ON MY YEARS BE-
tween wars, I have led such a fortunate life, I just had to
touch on some of the highlights. I can truthfully say that, if I
had to live my life over again, I wouldn't change a day of
it—well, maybe one or two. God forbid that I'd ever have to
give up either, but if I had to give up my direct-descent
membership in the Society of the Cincinnati or my Marine
Corps good conduct medal, it would have to be the

former—purely and simply because I inherited the first and earned the second. In case you may not know what the Society of the Cincinnati is (and too many people don't), I'll tell you.

Shortly after the American War of Independence, the society was founded by George Washington, who patterned it after Julius Caesar's Order of Cincinnatus. The society's original members comprised officers who had served under Washington's command for three years or more in the Revolution. Their membership was passed down to their eldest son, and so on down the line. However, around 1940, so many members had passed away leaving no male descendant that the ranks of the society had thinned to the point that the hereditary rule was changed to allow a member to name as his successor his nearest male relative. For instance, I have no son or brother, so I named my eldest male first cousin on my father's side of the family as my successor. As he died recently, I have now named his eldest son.

There is a state society in each of the original states and one in France. Presently there are approximately 2,400 members, about as many as there can ever be. John O'Hara once told me that one of his ancestors had been an officer in the Revolution and wondered if he was eligible for membership in the society. Later he found out that his ancestor had been a British officer! End of aspiration.

Once I heard of a chap who, when asked what the Society of the Cincinnati was, replied that it was a group in Cincinnati, Ohio, that had something to do with the Revolution! Actually, the first governor-general of the northwest province and an original member of the society, gave the City of Cincinnati its name. Originally, it was a small town called Losantiville, on the Ohio River, opposite the mouth of the Licking River. Enough of that!

Getting militarily involved with another pip-squeak country so shortly after our uncalled-for defense of South Korea proved conclusively that the United States had learned nothing from the Korean debacle.

Joe Foss and myself, 1962

As I watched, on television, Marines having a tough time of it in Vietnam, I got madder and madder. I was knocking back old-fashioneds and got so mad I ended up drinking straight bourbons. This fact, probably, had a lot to do with my typing a formal letter to Marine Corps Headquarters requesting recall to active duty. In the letter, I admitted I was a bit old and suggested that possibly I could take on a desk job, thereby relieving a younger man for combat duty.

I mailed the letter that same evening, and the following morning when I remembered what I'd done, I immediately started practicing limping. However, I didn't have to practice for very long, because within a week I received a reply. The Marine Corps expressed their thanks to me for offering my services and went on to say that they were sorry, but retired officers were being called back only to sit on promotion boards.

Being turned down bothered me none at all, but what some bum had written in longhand across the bottom of the reply did. In large letters was written, "And Ben—you know you are too damn old." I still say it was a bum who wrote it. But, you know, goddammit! he was right.

Through the years, I have sincerely believed three things: "What is to be, will be." "When your number's up, you're going." "Only Suckers Worry." And don't think that those beliefs didn't help me a lot during my war years. In combat, I tried to sell myself on another: "Nothing is ever as serious as it seems at the moment."

Not that anybody gives a damn, but, if I were ever asked what was the most memorable sight I can remember, I'd have to say it was my first glimpse of the Statue of Liberty from the deck of a hospital ship as I was returning to my homeland after World War I.

I sincerely hope that I haven't given the impression that my behavior in the Corps was typical of all Marines, because it wasn't. As a Marine reserve I got away with things a Marine regular wouldn't have dared attempt. And, I was fortunate—fortunate that in World War I, I was too young to care; in World War II, too old to worry; and fortunate that I was given no tough assignments in Korea. I can easily understand how this book could cause a U.S. Marine regular to wonder if perhaps I hadn't served in some other Marine Corps. However, be that as it may, I still maintain that be they reserves or be they regulars: once a Marine—always a Marine.

INDEX OF PEOPLE, PLACES, THINGS

Italic numbers refer to illustrations.